ST. VINCENT AND THE GRENADINES TRAVEL GUIDE 2024

A Dream Destination for Nature Lovers: Your Comprehensive Handbook to Explore Caribbean Islands, Discovering the Beauty and The Natural Wonders.

Victoria J Barham

Copyright © [2024] by [Victoria J Barham].

All rights reserved. No part of this publication may be reproduced, distributed, or transmitted in any form or by any means, including photocopying, recording, or other electronic or mechanical methods, without the prior written permission of the publisher, except in the case of brief quotations embodied in critical reviews and certain other noncommercial uses permitted by copyright law.

Table of content

INTRODUCTION
  Overview of St. Vincent and the Grenadines
  Brief History and Cultural Background
CHAPTER 1. Planning Your Trip
  Best Time to Visit
  Visa Requirements and Entry Information
  Packing Checklist
  Currency and Budgeting Tips
  Health and Safety Considerations
CHAPTER 2. Getting There and Around
  Flight Options and Major Airports
  MAP
  Inter-Island Transportation
  Renting Cars and Local Transport
CHAPTER 3. Accommodations
  Hotels and Resorts
  Booking your Hotel and Resort
CHAPTER 4. Exploring St. Vincent
  Must-Visit Attractions

- Historical Landmarks
- Outdoor Activities and Adventure
- Local Markets and Shopping

CHAPTER 5. Island Hopping in the Grenadines
- Overview of Grenadine Islands
- Choosing Your st Vincent's Island Itinerary
  - A 3 Days Itinerary
  - A 5 Days Itinerary
  - A 7 Days Itinerary
- Transportation Between Islands
- Unique Experiences on Each Island

CHAPTER 6. Beaches and Water Activities
- Top Beaches in St. Vincent and the Grenadines
- Snorkeling and Diving Spots
- Sailing and Water Sports

CHAPTER 7. Cuisine and Dining
- Local Culinary Delights
- Popular Restaurants and Eateries
- Dining Etiquette and Tips

CHAPTER 8. Cultural Experiences
- Traditional Festivals and Events

- Arts and Crafts
- Interacting with Locals

CHAPTER 9. Practical Tips
- Communication and Language
- Electricity and Plug Types
- Sustainable Travel Practices

CHAPTER 10. Photography and Filming
- Scenic Spots for Capturing Memories
- Respectful Photography Guidelines

CHAPTER 11. St. Vincent and the Grenadines in Every Season
- Seasonal Highlights and Events

Conclusion

INTRODUCTION

I was immersed in the vibrant tapestry of St. Vincent and the Grenadines, beneath an azure sky and cotton-white clouds. As we embarked on our journey, we were met with the promise of unforgettable adventures and tropical delights.

As the plane touched down at Argyle International Airport, I was impressed by the beautiful green islands that dot the pure Caribbean Sea like emeralds. I was lured to St. Vincent and the Grenadines because of its beautiful beaches and volcanic terrain.

Bequia, the largest of the Grenadines, is where I first discovered the charm of these islands.

Bequia, with its turquoise oceans sparkling in the sun, welcomed me with open arms as it snuggled within Admiralty Bay. The bustling businesses and attractive cafés along the busy Belmont Walkway hinted to the rich cultural tapestry that awaited discovery.

Bequia's beaches have an irresistible allure. Lower Bay, a crescent of white beach surrounded by calm waves, served as my retreat for the day. I gazed out to the horizon, where the sea and sky danced in perfect harmony, and surrendered in to the calming beat of the waves.

I went snorkeling at Princess Margaret Reef's crystal-clear waters because I wanted to view the underwater riches. A kaleidoscope of marine life emerged underneath me, including brilliant coral gardens, frolicking sea turtles, and schools of tropical fish that painted the ocean floor with nature's vibrant color pallet. The rhythmic motion of the watery environment will always leave an impression on my memory.

I sailed from Bequia to the calm Tobago Cays, a marine sanctuary where time seemed to have stopped. Snorkelers and divers sought sanctuary in the clear waters, which revealed a world of brilliant coral reefs and diverse marine life. As I swam beside graceful manta rays and gentle nurse sharks, I was stunned by the undisturbed beauty of this underwater sanctuary.

I was on the dunes of Salt Whistle Bay on Mayreau, a small island with a big heart, as the sun sank. The peaceful ambiance of this secluded refuge was reflected in the sky, which was painted in delicate pink and orange hues. A local steel drum band provided the evening's music, with pieces that reflected the Caribbean's impassioned tempo.

Exploring the main island of St. Vincent proved to be an adventure through lush jungles and stunning volcanic landscapes. Mist enveloped the La Soufrière volcano, creating an eerie atmosphere. I went into deep jungle with a knowledgeable local, learning about the island's unique flora and fauna while also discovering secret waterfalls.

I strolled onto the Pirates of the Caribbean sets in the picturesque town of Wallilabou, where the film's renowned ships remained afloat. The sea wind murmured stories of daring deeds, giving my journey a sense of magical cinematography.

My favorite aspect of my trip to St. Vincent was being immersed in Garifuna culture. The frenzied dance routines at the Garifuna Heritage Center, along with the villagers' drumming noises, made for a spectacular encounter. Through engagement with the community, I learned about their rituals and history, as well as the resilience of individuals who are deeply anchored in their past.

As my trip to St. Vincent and the Grenadines came to an end, I found consolation in Mustique's understated beauty. Mustique, noted for its remoteness and beautiful beaches, offered an affluent sanctuary amidst the Caribbean's natural beauty. Beyond its opulent homes, the island enticed me to stroll along calm beaches and admire breathtaking sunsets over the turquoise ocean.

When I reflected on my time in St. Vincent and the Grenadines, I realized that the islands' allure was attributable not just to their beautiful landscape, but also to the kind people who greeted and welcomed me into their vibrant communities. Every moment became a brushstroke in a picture of memories, from Bequia's busy streets to Mustique's tranquil beaches, a testament to the Caribbean paradise's eternal beauty.

Overview of St. Vincent and the Grenadines

A little island republic in the southern Caribbean Sea is called St. Vincent and the Grenadines. It consists of thirty-two islands and

cays, the biggest and most populated of which is St. Vincent. The nation is home to over 110,000 people and has a total land area of 389 square kilometers.

Kingstown, the capital, is situated on St. Vincent island. The Eastern Caribbean dollar is the unit of currency, and English is the official language.

The year-round temperatures of St. Vincent and the Grenadines, which are tropical, range from 24 to 30 degrees Celsius. Bananas are the largest export crop, and agriculture accounts for the majority of the nation's GDP. A significant sector in the nation is tourism, which draws tourists because of the stunning beaches, vibrant jungles, and coral reefs.

The nation has a diverse range of cultural traditions, shaped by the African, European, and native Carib peoples. A significant aspect of the culture is music, dancing, and festivals; calypso and soca music are especially well-liked.

Both the Commonwealth of Nations and the United Nations recognize St. Vincent and the Grenadines as a member. It is also a part of the Organization of Eastern Caribbean States (OECS) and the Caribbean Community (CARICOM).

Brief History and Cultural Background

A country in the Lesser Antilles group, Saint Vincent and the Grenadines is located where the Caribbean Sea meets the Atlantic Ocean on its eastern edge. The main island of Saint Vincent and the northern two thirds of the Grenadines, a series of smaller islands that stretches south from Saint Vincent to Grenada, make up its 389 square kilometer (150 sq mi) area.

History of Saint Vincent and the Grenadines

The Carib Indians called the island that is now known as Saint Vincent "Hairouna" at first. Up to the 18th century, Carib Indians resisted European colonization in St. Vincent with great violence. Around that time, former slaves from Africa who had either run away or been shipwrecked and sought safety in mainland St. Vincent after fleeing Barbados, St. Lucia, and Grenada, intermarried with the Caribs and were known as Garifuna or Black Caribs.

After taking over the island in 1719, French colonists planted plantations where they produced sugar, cotton, tobacco, coffee, and indigo. Africans held in slavery labored on these plantations. France gave Britain the authority of St. Vincent in 1763. But in 1779, France returned to conquer the island.

Once they touched down at Calliaqua, close to Fort Duvernette, the French took back control. With the signing of the Treaties of Versailles in 1783, the British eventually reclaimed St. Vincent. These agreements served as supplemental agreements to the Treaty of Paris (1783), which allowed Great Britain to formally acknowledge the American Revolution's conclusion.

There was fighting between the British and the Black Caribs, under the leadership of the intrepid Paramount Chief Joseph Chatoyer, between 1783 and 1796. The open battle came to an end in 1796 when British General Sir Ralph Abercromby put down a rebellion that the radical Frenchman Victor Hugues had instigated. Eventually, more than 5,000 Black Caribs were sent to the Honduran island of Roatan.

In 1834, slavery was outlawed in Saint Vincent. A term of apprenticeship ensued, culminating in 1838. Following its conclusion, the plantations had a labor shortage, which was originally filled by the importation of indentured slaves.

Many Portuguese immigrants came from Madeira in the late 1840s, while shiploads of laborers from East India arrived between 1861 and 1888. The world's sugar prices were so low that the economy remained stagnant until the turn of the century, meaning that conditions remained terrible for both immigrant agricultural laborers and former slaves.

Under the British, St. Vincent went through many phases of colonial status from 1763 until gaining independence in 1979. 1776 saw the authorization of a representative assembly; 1877 saw the establishment of Crown Colony governance; 1925 saw the creation of a legislative council; and 1951 saw the implementation of universal adult suffrage.

The British attempted in vain to unite St. Vincent with other Windward Islands on many occasions while they controlled the island. With a single government, this would have made Britain's authority over the area easier.

Several British-controlled regional islands, notably St. Vincent, also independently attempted to unite in the 1960s. The goal of the union, which was to be named the West Indies Federation, was to be free of British domination. The 1962 effort was a failure.

On October 27, 1969, Britain bestowed "associate statehood" status for St. Vincent. This was not quite independence, but it did give St. Vincent total authority over its internal affairs. The last of the Windward Islands to achieve independence was St. Vincent and the Grenadines, which did so on October 27, 1979, as a result of a referendum led by Milton Cato. On the tenth anniversary of St. Vincent's associate statehood, the country gained independence.

The history of the nation has been marked by natural calamities. 2,000 people were killed when the La Soufriere volcano erupted in 1902. The economy declined and a large amount of farmland was destroyed. La Soufriere erupted once more in April 1979. Again, there was significant agricultural damage, and many had to be evacuated even though nobody was killed. Hurricanes in 1980 and 1987 damaged farms of coconuts and bananas. Extremely active hurricane seasons also occurred in 1998 and 1999, with Hurricane Lenny in 1999 severely damaging the island's west shore.

Voters were requested to accept a new constitution on November 25, 2009, which would replace Queen Elizabeth II as head of state with a President and turn the nation into a republic. The requisite two-thirds majority was not reached, as 29,019 votes (55.64 percent) were cast against 22, 493 votes (43.13%). The nation then celebrated, with almost 10,000 guests attending a reception in Kingstown, the nation's capital.

The economy of Saint Vincent and the Grenadines

The most significant industry in this lower-middle-income economy is agriculture, which is dominated by the production of bananas. The services sector is also significant, mostly due to the expanding tourism industry. The government's efforts to bring in new industries have not been very effective, and the high unemployment rate of 22% persists. The main hindrance to the islands' growth is their continued reliance on a single crop. Significant sections of crops were destroyed by tropical storms in 1994 and 1995.

There is a great deal of room for growth in the tourist industry over the next 10 years. The island has been the site of recent Pirates of the Caribbean filming, which has increased tourism and increased awareness of the nation abroad. Strong activity in the building industry and an uptick in tourism have spurred recent development.

With the new international airport now under development, an additional boost is anticipated. There are two little industries: manufacturing and offshore finance, whose very stringent secrecy requirements have drawn attention from throughout the world. In addition, under IWC subsistence limits, Bequian natives are allowed to kill up to four humpback whales annually.

The culture of Saint Vincent and the Grenadines

The musical styles of Saint Vincent and the Grenadines include reggae, big drum, calypso, soca, and steelpan. Traditional storytelling, string band music, and bele and quadrille music are also well-liked. Written by Phyllis Joyce McClean Punnett and with music by Joel Bertram Miguel, "St Vincent Land So Beautiful" was selected as the national anthem of Saint Vincent and the Grenadines in 1979 upon the country's independence. Marlon Roudette, main vocalist of Mattafix, is the most well-known St. Vincentian singer abroad. Famously, the band's popular song "Big City Life" peaked at number one on charts in Austria, Germany, Italy, New Zealand, Poland, and Switzerland.

Bomani, Maddzart, Skarpyon, Jamesy P, Kevin Lyttle ("Turn Me On"), and Alston "Becket" Cyrus ("Teaser") are among the other vocalists. Most famously, Problem Child advanced to the 2008 carnival Soca monarch finals in Trinidad and Tobago after winning the local carnival Road March in July 2007 with his smash song "Party Animal". Skakes Studio, JR Studios, Sky Studio, and Non-fiction Recordings are some of St. Vincent's recording studios.

Saint Vincent and the Grenadines: Government, legislation, and political structure

Within the Commonwealth of Nations, Saint Vincent and the Grenadines is a parliamentary democracy and constitutional monarchy led by Queen Elizabeth II, who is referred to as Queen of Saint Vincent and the Grenadines. The Governor General of Saint Vincent and the Grenadines, presently Sir Frederick Ballantyne, represents the Queen in the nation; the Queen does not live on the islands.

The majority of the Governor General's duties are ceremonial in nature, such as appointing different government officials and kicking off the House of Assembly on the islands. The elected prime minister and his or her cabinet are in charge of the government. The greatest minority shareholder in general elections forms a legislative opposition led by the opposition leader. The Honorable Dr. Ralph Gonsalves is the prime minister in office right now.

Although the Royal Saint Vincent and the Grenadines Police Force has a Special Service Unit, the nation does not have an official armed forces.

The Organization of Eastern Caribbean States (OECS), ALBA, and the Caribbean Community (CARICOM) all recognize Saint Vincent and the Grenadines as full and active members.

CHAPTER 1. Planning Your Trip

Best Time to Visit

Your choices for weather, activity, and crowd density will all play a role in determining when is the ideal time to visit St. Vincent and the Grenadines. The two major seasons of the islands' tropical climate are the rainy season (June to November) and the dry season (December to May). Here's a summary to aid with your planning:

December to May is the dry season.
- Because of the pleasant weather, this time of year is regarded as the busiest travel season.
- Anticipate high temperatures, plenty of sunlight, and a decreased likelihood of rain.
- Perfect for outdoor excursions, diving, snorkeling, and beach sports.

- There is a greater demand for lodging, therefore making reservations in advance is advised.

Rainy Season: June through November
- Rainfall is heavier during this season, and there is a greater likelihood of hurricanes or tropical storms, particularly from August to October.
- Even though there may be brief, intense downpours on the islands, the flora always grows lush and colorful.
- There can be fewer visitors at this time, making the rooms more affordable.
- If you decide to go during the rainy season, be prepared for possible weather-related delays.

Particular Points to Remember:
- **Hurricane Season:** Although hurricanes do not impact St. Vincent and the Grenadines as often as they do other Caribbean locations, it is still important to be aware of when the hurricane season peaks, which runs from August to October. It is important to get travel insurance at this time.
- **Events and Festivals:** Consult the schedule if you're curious in the customs and traditions of the area. The annual carnival of St. Vincent, called Vincy Mas, generally happens in June or July.

Individual Preferences:
- Think about the activities and weather that you enjoy. The dry season may be better if you value bright, dry weather above all else for activities like water

sports and relaxing on beaches. If you like lush scenery and don't mind the odd downpour, the rainy season may be a memorable experience.

Your priorities will determine the ideal time to go to St. Vincent and the Grenadines. The rainy season might provide beautiful vistas and a more sedate ambiance, while the dry season offers the best weather. If you are planning a vacation during hurricane season, be sure to check the weather forecast and any possible interruptions to your travel schedule.

Visa Requirements and Entry Information

We are speaking about Saint Vincent and the Grenadines, an island in the Caribbean Sea that is a picture-perfect paradise that is adored by visitors, residents, artists, billionaires, and everyone else who has the opportunity to come.

Thus, if you're someone looking for adventure, you should think about obtaining a visa for Saint Vincent and the Grenadines so that you may go to this amazing island.

For Saint Vincent and the Grenadines, Who Needs a Visa?

Before visiting Saint Vincent and the Grenadines, nationals of the following countries must apply for a visa:

[Afghanistan, Iraq, China, Lebanon, Dominican Republic, Nigeria, Haiti, Palestine, Iran and Syria](#)

For a period of six months, citizens of the following nations may visit and stay in Saint Vincent and the Grenadines without a visa:

Bahamas, Guinea, Tobago and Trinidad, Barbados, Jamaica, United Kingdom, Belize, Suriname, Canada, United States and Taiwan

Visas are not required for citizens of the other nations mentioned below to visit and remain in Saint Vincent and the Grenades for 90 days within a 180-day period:

Every citizen of the EU (except from those in Ireland), Norway, Ukraine, Iceland, Russia, United Arab Emirates, Liechtenstein and Switzerland

The following nations' citizens are allowed to travel to Saint Vincent and the Grenades:

Barbuda, Antigua, Dominican Republic, Grenada, Saint Lucia and Saint Kitts and Nevis

Visa categories for St. Vincent and the Grenadines

Visas for Saint Vincent and the Grenadines come in a variety of forms, including:

- a visa for transit.
- a temporary visa.
- a visa for an extended stay.
- a visa for immigrants.
- a visa for humanitarian purposes.

Visa Requirements for Saint Vincent and the Grenadines

In order to apply for a visa to Saint Vincent and the Grenadines, you need to provide the following paperwork:

- a copy of the bio page from a current passport.

- an application for a visa to the Saint Vincent and the Grenadines that is filled out and signed.
- an invitation letter from a friend or family member.
- a criminal history record certificate from your national government.
- An applicant's and your sponsor's bank document statement (if applicable).
- Evidence of lodging in St. Vincent and the Grenadines.
- A charter arrangement, if relevant.

How Do I Apply for a Visa to the Grenadines and St Vincent?

The procedures to apply for a visa to Saint Vincent and the Grenadines are as follows:

- assemble the necessary paperwork for a visa to Saint Vincent and the Grenadines.

- Send the necessary paperwork to Saint Vincent and the Grenadines' Ministry of National Security by postal mail.
- The visa application for Saint Vincent and the Grenadines must be completed.
- Await the reply.

How Much Time Do I Have With a Visa to Enter Saint Vincent and the Grenadines?

A Saint Vincent and the Grenadines visa typically lasts for one month. Nonetheless, visitors with British passports or British nationals living abroad are permitted a six-month stay in the nation.

Note: OECS countries are welcome to remain in Saint Vincent and the Grenades for an extended period of time. However, in order to remain in the nation, individuals must demonstrate their ability to support themselves financially and that they are stable.

Visa fees for Saint Vincent and the Grenadines

A $200 visa cost must be paid in full at the time of applying for a Saint Vincent and the Grenadines passport. The Accountant General, Treasury Department, Kingstown, St. Vincent is where you may complete the fee payment.

However, there is still a final payment of $96.00 that the applicant has to make for the wire transfer.

Saint Vincent and the Grenadines residency permit

A Saint Vincent and the Grenadines temporary residency visa may be applied for by anybody planning to remain in the country for more than a year. You may apply for a permanent residence permit if you have been in the nation for seven years on a temporary resident visa.

You must compile and provide the necessary paperwork to the Office of the Prime Minister (Residency Department) in order to apply for a residence permit in Saint Vincent and the Grenadines.

Note: Depending on the kind of residence permit you ask for (permanent or temporary), you must pay a specified sum when applying for one.

Why Travel to the Grenadines and St Vincent?

You may unwind and spend a few days away from the outside world in an amazing location with stunning views and fantastic beaches. Here are some more explanations for traveling to the enchanted Saint Vincent and the Grenadines:

- You may explore a number of exquisite gardens and, for a little fee, hire a guide to give you a tour of the area and its background.
- You may go to Bequia for the day and spend some time there.
- You could go scuba diving.
- A cheap boat journey can take you to a variety of fantastic beaches.
- Everything you need may be found in Kingstown's fantastic marketplace.
- You may spend the whole day in Mustique and go celebrity spotting. A variety of artists, pop stars, actors, etc. frequent the location.

- Relaxing at a spa may be a great way to treat yourself and have an excellent day.
- There are natural ocean swimming pools.
- In addition to having a great time in the water, you may witness other marine animals, like dolphins and whales.

Packing Checklist

Take into account the tropical weather and the activities you want to partake in while packing for St. Vincent and the Grenadines. The following basic packing list will assist you in getting ready for your trip:

Clothes:
- Clothing that is airy and lightweight (sundresses, T-shirts, shorts).
- Swimwear for activities at the beach.
- light-colored long sleeves and trousers to defend against the sun.
- Dress comfortably for an evening meal out.
- sandals or cozy walking shoes.
- sea shoes for activities in the sea and coral beaches.
- For sun protection, use a hat and sunglasses.

Environment-Related Items:
- SPF-high sunscreen.
- repellent for insects.
- lightweight poncho or rain jacket (particularly in the rainy season).

- umbrella suitable for travel.

Essentials for Travel:
- Travel papers and passports.
- insurance for travel.
- Photocopies and personal identity.
- Electronic chargers and power adapters.
- lightweight daypack suitable for travel.

Well-being and Personal Cleanliness:
- A copy of the prescription and any prescribed drugs.
- Simple first aid package (bandages, antiseptic, analgesics).
- personal hygiene products.

Wet wipes and hand sanitizer.
Electronics:
- A camera or smartphone to record moments in time.

- An electronic bag or pouch that is waterproof.
- portable power bank/charger.

Activities on the Beach and in the Water:
- Snorkeling equipment (if you possess any).
- Beach towel or thin towel for traveling.
- a phone cover that is waterproof.
- a dry bag at the beach to keep valuables safe.

Other:
- Money in cash and debit/credit cards.
- maps or travel guides.
- Any specialized gear (like hiking boots or binoculars) needed for the scheduled activities?

Records:
- Printed travel schedule and hotel bookings.
- Details for emergency contacts.

Extra Items:
- Travel hammock that's lightweight.
- Pillow for travel.
- certification for diving or snorkeling, if you want to dive.

Don't forget to modify this checklist according to your unique requirements, the length of your visit, and the things you want to do. Additionally, be sure to look for any health and safety regulations or travel warnings, particularly in light of the current world situation.

Currency and Budgeting Tips

The Eastern Caribbean Dollar (EC$) is the accepted form of payment. In St. Vincent and the Grenadines, the US dollar is also commonly used, and the exchange rate is set at US$1 = EC$2.68%. There are fluctuations in exchange rates while dealing with foreign currencies.

Credit cards are accepted at many hotels, restaurants, and establishments. Carrying cash on trips is advised, since some smaller eateries and establishments only accept cash.

Typically, the cost of a one-person vacation to Saint Vincent and the Grenadines is $1,159 (EC$3,132) and for two persons, it is $2,318 (EC$6,263). This covers lodging, meals, local transit, and sightseeing.

The average cost of a two-week vacation to Saint Vincent and the Grenadines is $2,318 (EC$6,263) for an individual and $4,635 (EC$12,527) for a couple. This price covers lodging, meals, local transit, and touring.

Note that pricing might change depending on your pace, manner of travel, and other factors. When traveling as a family of three or four, the cost per person generally decreases since shared hotel accommodations and lower tickets for children are available. Over an extended duration of slower travel, your daily budget will decrease as well. A couple spending a month in Saint Vincent and the Grenadines together may often spend less per day per person than a single individual visiting for a week.

The average cost of a one-month vacation to Saint Vincent and the Grenadines is around

$4,966 (EC$13,422) for individuals and $9,933 (EC$26,843) for groups of two. The daily cost will rise as you visit more locations since transportation expenses will rise.

US Dollars: Some establishments in tourist regions could take US dollars. To prevent bad exchange rates, it is advised to do transactions using Eastern Caribbean Dollars.

Tips for Budgeting:

Using Cash and Credit Cards:
- For convenience, carry both cash and credit cards.
- Most bigger facilities, including restaurants and hotels, accept major credit cards.

ATMs:
- Urban locations have access to ATMs. To prevent any problems using your cards overseas, let your bank know about your trip schedule.
- Take out money in Eastern Caribbean Dollars to cover minor costs.

Regional Markets:
- For snacks and fresh veggies, visit your local markets. They often provide a genuine and reasonably priced dining experience.

Dining:
- Look at nearby restaurants for tasty and reasonably priced meals. Enjoying the cuisine of the area via street food might be a terrific idea.

Accommodations:
- The price of lodging might change. To fit your budget, take into account a combination of guesthouses, hotels, and vacation rentals.
- Getting a reservation in advance might lead to lower prices.

Transport:
- There is access to public transit, which may be a reasonably priced means of traveling.
- For traveling to farther-flung locations, renting a vehicle could be practical.

Activities:
- Like beaches and hiking paths, many natural sites are free or charge a small admission fee.

- Water sports like diving and snorkeling may come with an expense.

Tipping:
- In St. Vincent and the Grenadines, leaving a tip is expected. Some restaurants include a service fee on bills, but extra gratuities are welcomed, particularly for excellent service.

Communication:
- To save hefty roaming costs, think about getting your phone a local SIM card. This lowers the expense of staying connected.

Security and Safety:
- For valuables, use the hotel safes.
- When utilizing an ATM, use caution and attempt to use them in places that are safe and well-lit.

Keep in mind that these are just approximate estimates, and that actual expenses may differ depending on your own tastes and the places you visit. It's a good idea to keep an eye out for any revisions or travel warnings and adjust your budget appropriately.

Health and Safety Considerations

Crime

Pickpocketing and handbag snatching are examples of minor crimes that happen, especially in larger cities like Kingstown. Thefts from moored and docked boats fall under this category. Theft targets include cash, outboard engines, and personal goods.

Though uncommon, violent crime does happen.
- Make sure that everything you own, such as your passport and other travel papers, is always safe.
- Keep a photocopy of your passport's identifying page with you at all times.
- Never leave valuables unattended, particularly on beaches or in cars, including cash, credit cards, and devices.
- Avoid carrying a lot of cash.
- When using ATMs, use caution, particularly after nightfall.
- Traveling between and via the eastern Caribbean islands at night should be

avoided since these places may be dangerous and robbed of their valuables.

Activities involving water
- Seas near the coast may be hazardous. Rips happen often.
- Not every beach has caution signs or lifeguards on duty.
- Swimming should be done with care, particularly at Mount Wynne, Trinity Falls, and Rawacou.
- Avoid swimming alone, after hours, and beyond designated zones.
- Talk to locals and tour guides about potential risks and places to swim safely.
- Observe the guidance provided by local authorities.

If you engage in any aquatic sports:
- Put on the proper safety gear, such helmets and life jackets.
- certify that the necessary equipment is on hand and in working order.

Hiking

The northern region of Saint Vincent Island, which includes Trinity Falls, La Soufrière, and the Falls of Baleine, has a sparse police presence. When hiking in these places, use care.

If you plan to go hiking:
- Never do this alone; instead, always use a qualified guide from a respectable business.
- Purchase travel insurance that covers medical evacuation and helicopter rescue.

- make sure your physical state is sufficient to handle the demands of your activity.
- make sure you have the right gear and are knowledgeable about the weather and other factors that might be dangerous.
- Tell a friend or family member about your plans, including when you plan to return to camp.
- Before you go, get thorough information on the hiking routes; stay on designated paths.

Exhibitions

Demonstrations might happen. Violent outbursts may occur during even nonviolent protests. They may also cause traffic and public transit to be disrupted.

- Steer clear of protest and large-scale gathering locations.

- Observe the guidance provided by local authorities.
- Keep an eye on your local media for updates on the continuing protests.

Traffic safety

All over the nation, the state of the roads and traffic safety are typically satisfactory. Mountain roads are steep and winding, with few signage or guardrails. Hazards include potholes, speed bumps, and dim illumination.

Many times, drivers speed excessively.
There are few options for roadside help.
- When driving, especially after dark, use caution.
- If a pedestrian flags you down, don't stop since they could try to rob you.
- Always be mindful of your surroundings while you're a pedestrian.

Public conveyance

Taxi

In general, taxis are safe. Although they are not metered, most destinations have set charges.

- Seek out cabs with the window displaying the phrase "tourism approved."
- Before leaving, check the fare with the driver.

Buses

Buses are readily available and generally safe, however they may be crammed with people and move quickly.

Ferrets

Between Saint Vincent and Bequia, there is a reliable and secure ferry service.

Air travel

We don't evaluate if domestic foreign airlines are adhering to international safety regulations.

Well-being

Information on potential health hazards and ongoing or frequent restrictions in the destination is provided in this section. Take heed to this advice to reduce your chances of becoming sick while traveling. Not every danger is included here.

For tailored health advice and suggestions, speak with a medical practitioner or stop by a travel health clinic at least six weeks before your trip.

Regular immunizations

Regardless of where you're going, make sure your regular immunizations are current before you go. Check with your province or territory.

Measles, mumps, rubella (MMR), influenza, tetanus, pertussis, polio, varicella (chickenpox), and others are among the immunizations that fall under this category.

Pre-travel vaccinations and drugs

You run the danger of contracting avoidable illnesses while visiting this location. Consult a travel health specialist to find out whether vaccinations or drugs, depending on your schedule and location, may be appropriate for you.

Safe food and water practices

Consuming food or drinks tainted with bacteria, parasites, toxins, or viruses, as well as swimming or taking a bath in tainted water, may result in a number of ailments.

- When swimming or engaging in activities in freshwater (streams, canals, lakes), try to keep water out of your mouth, eyes, and nose, especially after a period of floods or severe rain. Even when water seems pure, it may nevertheless be tainted or poisoned.
- When taking a bath, taking a shower, or swimming in a pool or hot tub, avoid breathing in or ingesting water.

Preventing insect bites

The bites of infected insects, such as fleas, ticks, flies, or mosquitoes, may transmit a number of

illnesses. When visiting locations where there may be a possibility of contaminated insects:
- Apply bug spray or insect repellent to exposed skin.
- Wear loose, light-colored clothing made of fabrics with tight weaves, such polyester or nylon, to provide coverage.
- Reduce your exposure to insects
- When sleeping outside or in partially enclosed structures, use mosquito netting.

precautions for animals

Humans and animals may get some illnesses from one other, including influenza and rabies. You may be more likely to come into touch with animals if you travel through rural or wooded regions, go camping, go hiking, or visit wet markets, which are locations where live animals are killed and sold. You may also choose to explore caverns.

It is advised against consuming uncooked wild game and to stay away from animals such as dogs, cattle (pigs, cows), monkeys, snakes, rodents, birds, and bats.

Children should have close supervision since they are more prone to come into touch with animals.

Infections between individuals
If you're ill, stay at home and follow the correct cough and sneeze protocol, which calls for using a tissue or the bend of your arm rather than your hand. Lower your chance of getting the flu, colds, and other diseases by:
- Frequently wash your hands

- minimizing or avoiding spending a lot of time at large-scale events, crowded areas, or confined spaces (concerts, sports events, rallies)
- Keeping a safe distance from those who could be exhibiting signs of disease

Facilities and services for medicine

Major cities have access to high-quality medical treatment. In addition to the public hospitals in Georgetown and Bequia, there is one private and one public hospital in Kingstown. There are several clinics accessible as well.

In the event of a major disease or accident, medical evacuation may be necessary, however it might be very costly.

Make sure the travel insurance you purchase covers hospital stays and medical evacuations.

Remember this...

The traveler has the entire responsibility for the choice to travel. The traveler has sole responsibility for ensuring their own safety.

Get ready. When traveling, particularly if you will be leaving a big city center, don't anticipate the same quality of medical care as you would back home. Instead, bring a travel health kit.

CHAPTER 2. Getting There and Around

Flight Options and Major Airports

The main entry to the alluring Caribbean location of St. Vincent and the Grenadines is the Argyle International Airport (SVD). The archipelago provides a variety of airline alternatives for visitors and is well-connected to important international destinations.

Argyle International Airport (SVD)
Location:

On St. Vincent's eastern coast, close to the town of Argyle, is where you'll find Argyle International Airport. It serves as the primary international airport for the nearby Grenadine islands as well as St. Vincent.

Facilities:

1. Terminals: Argyle International Airport has a contemporary terminal with amenities for both local and international travel.

2. Airlines: Argyle International Airport is served by a number of domestic and international airlines.

3. Services: The airport offers necessary services such as facilities for customs and immigration as well as luggage handling.

Flight Options

Major International Airlines:
- There are flights to St. Vincent from international airlines including American Airlines, Delta, British Airways, and Air Canada. Depending on the airline and the location of departure, these trips often have one or more layovers.

Regional Airline:
- Caribbean airlines that provide easy connections to St. Vincent from nearby islands include LIAT (Leeward Islands Air Transport) and SVG Air. These regional planes provide a smooth means of visiting many Caribbean locations.

Connecting Flights:
- Connecting flights via important hubs like Miami, New York, London, or Toronto are an option for travelers. Connecting flights might be more cost-effective and provide you more freedom in selecting your departure location.

Exclusive Charters:
- If you want a more customized trip experience, you may hire a private

charter. For people traveling in groups or following certain itineraries, this option is very practical.

Travel Advice

1. Making a reservation in advance:
There may be a lot of demand for flights to St. Vincent, particularly during the busiest travel seasons. It is best to book your travel early in advance to guarantee your desired dates and affordable airfare.

2. Flexible Dates:
If your schedule permits, being flexible with your trip dates may help you find better offers. Mid-week flights often have lower demand.

3. Airport Transfers:

To guarantee a seamless ride from Argyle International Airport to your lodging, schedule your airport transfers in advance. The airport has rental automobiles and taxis available.

4. Verify Admission Requirements:

Verify entrance requirements—including visa laws and health precautions—before making a reservation to be sure you're following the most recent travel advisories.

Due to its many airline choices, St. Vincent and the Grenadines is accessible by tourists from all over the globe. The trip to this Caribbean paradise seems to be a smooth and captivating experience, regardless of your preference for direct international flights or connecting via regional airports.

BOOKING YOUR FLIGHT

There are many processes involved in booking a ticket to St. Vincent, from selecting your departure location to verifying your reservation. Here is a comprehensive how-to guide for booking a flight to St. Vincent:

Step 1: Planning and Research

1. Select the City of Departure:
- Decide the city or airport you want to leave from. Direct or connecting flights to St. Vincent are often available from major international airports such as Miami, New York, London, and Toronto.

2. Choose Your Travel Dates:
- Choose your trip dates taking into account the weather, local events, and your own schedule. If at all feasible, be

adaptable since changing your trip dates could result in more affordable possibilities.

3. Considering the Budget:
- Set aside money for the flight. Seasonality, the airline, and the time of booking may all affect prices. Think about signing up for travel notifications or comparing prices across other booking sites.

Step 2: Do A Web Search

1. Search engines for flights:
- Make use of well-known flight search engines such as Skyscanner, Kayak, or Google Flights. Put in your selected trip dates, departure city, and destination (St.

Vincent). Investigate various airlines and routes.

2. Websites for Airlines:
- Go to the official websites of the main carriers offering service to St. Vincent. Look for exclusive specials, discounts, and promotions that may not be found on other websites.

Step 3: Evaluate Your Options

1. Comparing Direct and Connecting Flights:
- Examine the benefits and drawbacks of direct vs connecting flights. While connecting flights may be more affordable but require a longer flight duration, direct flights tend to be more

convenient but may also be more expensive.

2. Examine the facilities:

- Think about the extras that various airlines provide, such seat selection, in-flight entertainment, and luggage allowance. This may affect how you travel in general.

Step 4: The Reservation Procedure

1. Select the Best Choice:

- Pick the flight choice that most closely matches your spending limit and preferences.

2. Book Through Airlines or Third-Party Platforms:

- Choose between making your reservation on the airline's website directly and via a third-party booking platform. Direct booking might give advantages and greater control, while third-party sites could have more affordable rates.

3. Enter the traveler's details:

- Input the necessary passenger data, such as names and contact information.

4. Select Seats and Extras:

- Select your seats as well as any other add-ons or services, such as seat upgrades or travel insurance, that are available at the time of booking.

Step 5: Payment and Confirmation

1. Examine the booking information:

- Verify again all the information on your reservation, such as the dates of travel, passenger count, and chosen choices.

2. Payment.
- Fill out your payment information to finish the reservation process. Make sure the payment option you use is reliable and safe.

3. Email Confirmation:
- Following payment, an email including your booking details, e-ticket, and other information should be sent to you. Please save this email for future use.

Step 6: Additional Considerations

1. Entry and Visa Requirements:

- Verify and meet any conditions for entrance or a visa to St. Vincent. Verify the most recent travel warnings and recommendations.

2. Transfers from the airport:
- Make travel arrangements to go from the airport to your St. Vincent lodging. If necessary, schedule transfers in advance.

You may quickly and easily book a ticket to St. Vincent by following these steps, which will guarantee a seamless and pleasurable beginning to your Caribbean vacation. Remain up to date on travel laws and take into account variables like affordability and adaptability while making reservations.

MAP

SCAN THE ABOVE QR CODE FOR YOUR MAKE

Inter-Island Transportation

The beautiful island archipelago of St. Vincent and the Grenadines provides a range of inter-island transportation choices, enabling visitors to experience the unique appeal of every location. This is a guide to St. Vincent's inter-island transportation:

1. Ferry Services

Grenadines Associated with:
- **Bequia Express:** Manages ferry services between Bequia and St. Vincent. The one-hour trip offers a picturesque ride across the Grenadines.
- Bequia, Canouan, and Union Island are connected to St. Vincent by the Grenadines Express. It offers a quick and easy way to go between these charming islands.

Public Ferries:
- A more affordable alternative are the public ferries that run between St. Vincent and several of the nearby Grenadines. It's best to check in advance since schedules sometimes change.

2. Exclusive Boat Rentals:

Yacht Services:
- Private yacht charters are available in St. Vincent and the Grenadines, which is well-known for its sailing-friendly seas. Charters for crewed or bareboats are available for travelers, giving them the freedom to visit many islands.

3. Air Travel:

SVG Air and Mustique Airways:
- Inter-island flights are provided by domestic carriers such as Mustique Airways and SVG Air. These brief flights provide a rapid and practical means of traveling between locations by linking St. Vincent to many Grenadine islands.

4. Water Taxis:

Individual Water Taxis:
- Private water taxis that provide individualized and efficient transportation between St. Vincent and nearby islands may be rented. For those looking for a more individualized and upscale vacation experience, this is the best choice.

5. Tips for Inter-Island Transportation:

Schedules and Reservations:
- Especially during the busiest travel seasons, check boat and aircraft schedules well in advance. If possible, make reservations to guarantee the time slot of your choice.

Considering the weather
- The weather may have an impact on boat and airline timetables, especially in the rainy season. Keep yourself updated on weather predictions and any possible delays.

Time of Travel:
- Travel times between islands might vary, so make appropriate plans. To maximize

your island-hopping experience, consider travel time while planning your schedule.

Flexible Itinerary:
- There are several beautiful islands to be found in St. Vincent and the Grenadines. Take into account a flexible schedule that will let you experience each place's own charm at your own leisure.

Health and Safety:
- Put safety first while traveling by water. Wear life jackets when required and abide with the safety instructions supplied by the ferry provider.

Advance Planning:
- Make early plans and reservations for inter-island transportation, particularly if you have certain trip dates or locations in

mind. This lessens last-minute difficulties and helps guarantee availability.

St. Vincent and the Grenadines offers a variety of inter-island transportation alternatives to suit different types of travelers, including boat, aircraft, ferry, and water taxi. As you make your way between these alluring Caribbean treasures, take in the azure seas and scenic vistas.

Renting Cars and Local Transport

By taxi is the most convenient method to get throughout St. Vincent and the Grenadines. On St. Vincent and the larger islands, taxis are widely available and reasonably priced for short distance travel. The quickest route from St. Vincent's E.T. Joshua Airport (SVD), which is a few miles southeast of Kingstown, to your accommodation is most likely to include taking a taxi. While renting a car is a possibility in St. Vincent, Bequia, and Mustique, it is not advised due to the challenging navigation of the islands' roadways. Although buses are another well-liked mode of transportation in St. Vincent, Bequia, and Union Island, they are sometimes crammed and stifling. Go to Kingstown, St. Vincent's primary port, to reach the Grenadines. Several ferry companies provide daily service between St. Vincent and the islands.

Major airports in St. Vincent and the Grenadines number five. The majority of travelers arrive at E.T. Joshua Airport (SVD), however smaller airstrips on Canouan (CIW), Bequia (BQU), Mustique (MQS), or Union Island (UNI) are all viable options.

Taxi

Along with some of the lesser isles, taxis may be found on the larger populous islands such as St. Vincent, Bequia, Mustique, and Union Islands. Since taxis are not metered, haggle over a fare before you get in your car. The approximate cost of the journey from E.T. Joshua Airport to downtown Kingstown is EC$30, or around $11.

Car

The winding roads of St. Vincent & The Grenadines are difficult to drive because of potholes, sharp bends, and hostile motorists. Remember that you must drive on the left side of the road if you're ready for a roadside adventure. A temporary local license, which you may get at the Revenue Office in Port Elizabeth, Bequia, or the police station on Bay Street in Kingstown, will also be required. You can obtain both of these documents at the police station. A temporary license is priced at $100EC, or around $40. Among the recommended automobile rental companies are Ben's Auto Rental and Avis.

Ferry

Every day, the Bequia Express departs from St. Vincent and travels round-trip to Bequia. Adult rates are EC$25, or around $10, while children's fares range from EC$15 to EC$20, or roughly $5 to $7. You should inquire with your lodging about boat transportation to the nearby islands. The easiest way to go island hopping is via boat, which your hotel could suggest renting.

Bus

Buses provide a convenient and reasonably priced means of transportation in St. Vincent if you don't want to deal with the headaches of renting an automobile. However, be ready for congested areas and sluggish moving traffic. From the seaside New Kingstown Fish Market, buses leave. The fare ranges from EC$1.50 (about $0.35) to EC$3 (about $1).

CHAPTER 3.
Accommodations

Hotels and Resorts

The top hotels in St. Vincent and the Grenadines have access to white-sand beaches, stunning vistas, and freshly caught seafood, whether they are situated on a private island or on the grounds of an ancient sugar plantation. You may anticipate everything from extravagant luxury to more family-friendly lodgings, along with opportunities for relaxation or adventure.

It would be understandable for first-timers to the eye-catching group of 33 islands known as St. Vincent and the Grenadines to not be familiar with many of the hotel names before their arrival. Although tourism has been there for a few decades, this former British colony in the Caribbean just gained independence in 1979 and has been sluggish to promote its attractions globally. Presently, meanwhile, the archipelago is home to an expanding portfolio, with islands such as picturesque Little Bequia seeing a surge in tourism, although in a very laid-back manner.

Wealthier guests have the option to reserve the whole resort for themselves, maybe with the goal of cruising their boats around the area, or they might treat themselves to villas on private islands. For everyone else, the option will be solitude in the verdant innards of the islands or relaxing on one of the stunning white sand beaches; just don't anticipate having to make any more urgent choices than that.

1. Bequia beach hotel, Bequia

Best for foodies

While there are many reasons to visit the Bequia Beach Hotel, dining at Bagatelle, the main restaurant, feels like the best one. It's doubtful that you'll quickly forget enjoying some freshly caught lobster and a bottle of white wine while watching the Caribbean waves break into Friendship Bay, which is just a few yards away. There are a number of different room classes available, with the estate villa being the largest. It has an infinity pool and, if all eight of its beds are occupied, provides surprisingly good value.

2. palm island resort and spa, palm island

Best for privacy
While there are more opulent resorts in the nation, few can compare to Palm Island Resort's unique offering of privacy, leisure, and adventure. It is characterized by palm palms and white sand beaches, and can be accessed after a ten-minute boat journey from Union

Island. The area has a turquoise sea halo. Even though the area has seen significant development since 1966, when it was still desolate, hiking and cycling are still possible there. The hotel offers a variety of all-inclusive packages in addition to rooms, suites, and villas.

3. Tropical hideaway boutique hotel, bequia

Best for a boutique break

The British proprietors of this hotel cannot be accused of misrepresenting their offering, despite the humorous generic nature of its name. With room for only 12 guests, it really qualifies as a boutique hotel; its tropical setting on Bequia is undeniable; nestled atop a hillside with a view of Admiralty Bay, it's also appropriate to characterize it as a hideaway.

The biggest of the three lodging choices is the hibiscus hut, which has a wide private veranda with a swinging chair for amazing views and a full-sized kitchen.

4. Mariners hotel, st vincent

Best for sailing

Yachts moored in its peaceful harbor often encircle the Mariner's Hotel, which has a jetty protruding like an accusing finger pointing toward Young Island. Inside, there are only 20 rooms (albeit not all of them offer those breathtaking views of the Caribbean). Situated in the southern region of the country's biggest island, Mariner's is well situated for both walking and taxi access to various pubs and restaurants. The on-site French Verandah, which serves French-inspired cuisine, is a short taxi ride from the botanical gardens.

5. Mandarin oriental canouan, canouan

Best for spa

You may be reassured that the brand has been quite controlled in its building if you are worried about the hospitality behemoth Mandarin Oriental existing on this little island. It definitely fits into the category of boutique hotels, but one that operates at the uppermost end, with only 26 suites and 13 villas. A portion of the 1,200 acres of the hotel backs onto an unusual golf course on the island, and it has its own private aircraft. In the meanwhile, luxurious Caribbean spa services are provided in over-the-water bungalows.

6. The liming, bequia

Best for weddings

The Liming, which resembles a Christmas tree hanging off the tip of Bequia's westernmost peninsula, specializes in custom-sized homes to accommodate your party. The biggest is the gingerlily mansion home, perfect for huge wedding parties since it has five en suite bedrooms, a kitchen, and its own private pool. It's advisable to accept their "art of doing nothing" since there isn't much else on this portion of the island and not much that can be reached on foot.

7. Bequia plantation hotel, bequia

Best for value

One of the greatest bargain hotels in St. Vincent and the Grenadines, this facility has spectacular sunsets from its west-facing Admiralty Bay location, direct beach access, and swinging coconut palms above. Even if the resort doesn't have a spa, there are still enough amenities for those who like to remain on site, and there are lots of things to keep you busy if you want to explore. You may easily go south to Princess Margaret Beach, which is well-known for its fantastic swimming and snorkeling, via the Belmont Boardwalk.

8. The cotton house, mustique

Best for couples

There are no other islands in the archipelago like the unique island of Mustique. After an unsuccessful attempt to develop it into a cotton plantation in the 1950s, it became a posh semi-private island that was well-liked by the British nobility. Today, the main hotel, the Cotton House, has only 17 rooms and a great bar and restaurant. There are also a number of villas available for those with the resources to locate their own tropical refuge.

9. Sugar Reef Bequia, Bequia

Best for adults only

Situated on a 65-acre coconut farm northeast of beautiful Bequia, Sugar Reef has a surprisingly diverse selection of only eight accommodations. Some are completely concealed by the dense foliage on the hillsides, while others let you go right out onto the beach at Industry Bay. The resort's cheap price point is belied by the seclusion it offers both there and elsewhere. While it's possible to go around the riotously green public spaces alone, you shouldn't be shocked to run upon other visitors in the turquoise waves.

10. Firefly Bequia Plantation, Bequia

Best for Solo Travellers

Firefly Bequia Plantation, complete with two on-site dogs, a charming six-hole golf course, and tours of the orchard, is very much on the eccentric side of the local hotel industry. Its audacious goal statement, "firefly is not for the boring, the pretentious, or the stuffy," is guaranteed to turn away the kind of customers who would find this place repulsive. If you're traveling to Bequia, don't miss the opportunity to try items manufactured on the site at the sea-salt tasting bar.

11. Spring Hotel, Bequia

Best for Families

With open-sided rooms and mosquito nets draped over four-poster beds, the Spring Hotel is a breezy affair, proudly situated at the more reasonably priced end of St. Vincent and the Grenadines hotel chain. Though there are many more opulent alternatives around the archipelago, few locations compare to this one for value and quality, with accommodations starting at less than £100 per night. If you want to delve further into your exploration, they can set you up with snorkeling excursions around the island or, if you'd like, full-day excursions out to the fascinating, deserted Tobago Cays.

12. Young island resort, young island

Best for watersports

Just barely, Young Island is one of the country's exclusive island resorts. Private water taxis may be booked at any time, and they take five minutes to travel the 200 yards to the main island of St. Vincent. The resort is set up around 29 different class-specific cottages, the nicest of which have their own plunge pools. Other attractions on the island include a spa, a pleasant stroll to the historic Duvernette Sea Fort, and the ability to arrange sailing and scuba diving trips.

13. Tenuta chatham bay, union island

Best for spotting wildlife

Union Island is a rare example of a west-facing all-inclusive resort since it receives much less traffic than the most of the populated islands to the north. This is not a mass-tourist monster you'll find elsewhere in the Caribbean, either, since there are just six well appointed homes and one restaurant. Look out for the uncommon, endemic union island gecko if you decide to explore the island on foot.

14. Petit saint vincent resort, petit saint vincent

Best for luxury

It's hard to imagine that petit saint vincent is a part of St. Vincent and the Grenadines, since there's only around 500 yards of azure ocean separating it from petite martinique, a Grenadian island. Despite their separate nationalities, they are both shielded by the same coral reef, which is fortunate since there is nothing but the Atlantic Ocean to the east of here. In contrast, the resort has two restaurants that are included in the accommodation cost due to the property's secluded location, and 21 cottages that are visited by personal butlers.

15. Salt Whistle Bay

Best for Beach Lovers

While the majority of the most opulent hotels in the Grenadines serve the one percent, Salt Whistle Bay on Mayreau provides a gloriously relaxed, yet no less exclusive, experience. Nestled inside one of the 22-acre property's eco-friendly bell tents or stone bungalows, each with brightly colored carpets, fans, and luxurious bedding, and strategically positioned to catch coastal breezes, you'll feel like a contemporary Robinson Crusoe. During the day, visitors may snorkel alongside sea turtles, sting rays, and exotic fish in the nearby reef-filled seas, and stand-up paddleboards and snorkeling masks are free of charge. Alternatively, they can try kiteboarding on the resort's dedicated beach. At night, have grilled lobster supper at the on-site restaurant and bar while chatting about your experiences.

Booking your Hotel and Resort

The procedure of making a hotel reservation on St. Vincent Island is simple. Here is a thorough, step-by-step guide to assist you with booking your lodging:

1. Planning and Research:

Specify Your Choices:
- Establish your spending limit, your ideal island location, and the kind of lodging you'll need (hotel, resort, or guesthouse).

Internet-Based Research:
- To investigate your alternatives, use online travel agents (OTAs) like Booking.com, Expedia, or Airbnb. To determine the caliber of the lodging, have a look at other passengers' evaluations.

2. Select Your Accommodation:

Filters Options:
- Use filters on booking platforms to narrow down your options based on price range, amenities, and guest ratings.

Examine the Policies:
- Verify the hotel's rules about payment options, cancellation policies, and any other pertinent information. Make sure the hotel of your choice fits your preferred style of travel.

3. The Reservations Process:

Choose the Room Type and Dates:
- Select the dates for your check-in and check-out. Choose the kind of room or suite that best meets your requirements.

Personal Information:

- Provide your name, contact information, and any special requests you may have along with your personal information.

Examine the booking information:
- Examine all booking information, including dates, kind of accommodation, and total amount, before confirming. Make sure everything is accurate.

4. Payment:

Options for Payment:
- Select your desired payment option, such as PayPal, credit/debit cards, etc. Verify the security of the payment procedure.

Look for deals or promotional codes:
- Check for any promo codes or discounts that could be applicable to your reservation. Certain booking sites provide unique bargains or loyalty programs.

5. Confirmation and Receipt:

Email Confirmation:
- An email confirming your payment should be sent to you. Your reservation number, booking details, and hotel contact details are all included in this email.

Save The Confirmation:
- Make a note of the reservation number and save the email confirmation. This is crucial for both the check-in process and any future correspondence with the hotel.

6. Additional Considerations:

Speak with the hotel:

- Consider contacting the hotel directly if you have any special requests or concerns. This might include asking for a certain room type, an early check-in time, or any other customized arrangements.

Verify Any Additional Fees:

- Be mindful of any potential extra costs, such as taxes or resort fees. Upon check-in, there may be certain costs to pay.

Examine the policies about cancellations:

- Learn about the cancellation policies of the hotel. Recognize the deadlines and any applicable cancellation penalties.

You may make a hotel reservation on St. Vincent Island with confidence by following these procedures, which will guarantee a relaxing and pleasurable stay on this Caribbean treasure.

CHAPTER 4. Exploring St. Vincent

Must-Visit Attractions

St. Vincent and the Grenadines is a boater's paradise, showcasing some of the Caribbean's most breathtaking landscapes. Stretching southward towards Grenada, this chain of thirty-six green volcanic islands has several white sand beaches and palm-lined harbors where large yachts moor alongside sailboats.

These are a lot of private islands, many with upscale resorts. There's great snorkeling only a short splash from shore, and many of the beaches are surrounded by coral reefs for diving. Skillful island explorers gravitate towards these serene and modest islands due to their traditional Caribbean landscapes and inherent charms, devoid of the hordes of visitors and cruise ship crowds typical of bigger ports.

Union Island serves as the southern entry point to the Grenadines, while Kingstown, the capital of St. Vincent, is known for its colonial architecture and cobblestone walkways.

The verdant islands of Bequia, Mustique, Mayreau, Canouan, Palm Island, and Petit St. Vincent are strewn over the surrounding waters like gems. Part of a marine park rimmed by coral reefs, the picture-perfect Tobago Cays are a favorite spot for snorkelers, divers, boaters, and beachcombers.

With our list of the top tourist destinations in St. Vincent and the Grenadines, you can choose the ideal spots to go.

1. The Cays of Tobago

The Tobago Cays, a group of five tiny, deserted islands in the southern Grenadines, are the focal point of the Tobago Cays Marine Park. Reefs shield the beaches, which provide quiet, clear seas for swimming and snorkeling. There is a wealth of marine life in the surrounding coral gardens.

Sea turtles may be seen by snorkelers and divers, along with stingrays, barracuda, and schools of reef fish.

One of the best things to do in St. Vincent & the Grenadines is take a day cruise to the Tobago Cays, where many boaters moor to enjoy the beaches and crystal-clear seas.

2. Botanical Gardens of St. Vincent

The charming St. Vincent Botanical Gardens are the oldest in the West Indies, having opened their doors in 1765.

Twenty acres of native and exotic tropical plants and trees, including hibiscus, cinnamon, nutmeg, mahogany, palms, and a breadfruit tree that is said to have sprouted from a seedling that Captain Bligh brought to the island, make up the gardens.

In a small aviary on the property, avian enthusiasts may see the native St. Vincent parrot. To get the most of these stunning gardens, pay a nominal price to hire a guide here at the gate.

Make sure to bring the kids along if you're traveling as a family. If you want to take a vacation from picking sand off other people's swimming clothes, this is the ideal location to go.

3. The Charlotte Fort

It's understandable why Fort Charlotte is among St. Vincent's most visited attractions. Constructed during the late 1700s and early 1800s, this ancient building is situated on a hill close to Edinboro. It offers breathtaking views of the Grenadines, Mt. St. Andrew, and Kingstown.

Originally intended to fend against ground invasions, the fort had more than thirty pieces of artillery and 600 people's worth of barracks. These days, the grounds still include the barracks, stone walls, and paintings in addition to a few cannons. To ensure that you have a proper tour, we recommend that you use the services of a local guide.

The hike to the fort is rather steep—roughly a forty-minute ascent—so be prepared for that. If the climb isn't your thing, take a bus to Edinboro, where the stroll will just take ten or so minutes.

4. The Volcano La Soufrière

Hiking to the crater of La Soufrière volcano, which should not be mistaken with La Grande Soufrière in Guadeloupe, is one of the most well-liked activities on the island of St. Vincent.

La Soufriere, at 1,234 meters above sea level, is the highest mountain on St. Vincent. The most recent eruption occurred in April 2021, indicating that it is still active.

Going on a guided trek is a popular option to climb to the peak. Along the trip, you'll witness cloud forest, rainforests, and breathtaking views of the surrounding countryside. You'll also learn about the specially adapted flora and animals. You'll have the opportunity to explore the crater after reaching the summit.

You may trek the leeward path, which takes six to eight hours round trip, or the more straightforward and well-trod windward trail, which takes three to four hours round trip, to get to the crater.

Take caution: this trip is not for the faint of heart because of the recent eruptions that have left the pathways rocky and uneven. Put on the proper shoes.

5. Bequia

Charming Bequia (pronounced "Beck-way") is a well-liked sailing resort and the second biggest of the Grenadines. Dappled with bougainvillea, verdant slopes cascade into bays teeming with boats. The island is renowned for being welcoming and safe as well.

The primary economic hub of the island, Port Elizabeth on Admiralty Bay, is one of the most visited locations on Bequia. On the south side of town, a boardwalk hugs the shore, passing charming tiny stores and eateries. To get some insight into the history of the island, pay a visit to the Bequia Maritime Museum.

Beaches in Bequia: Princess Margaret Beach is a picturesque beach accessible by a route over a short hill near Port Elizabeth's southern edge. Another length of golden sand beach with excellent snorkeling is Lower Bay, which is separated from this one by a rocky outcrop.

A visit to the Firefly Plantation is another well-liked activity in Bequia. You may wander around the verdant grounds and sample some of the fresh tropical fruits, such as guava, coconut, breadfruit, bananas, and mangos, that have been harvested from the trees. In addition, you may see the remnants of a sugar mill that dates back 280 years and crush sugar cane to produce your own juice.

6. Mayreau's Salt Whistle Bay

Only 2.5 square kilometers in size and home to Salt Whistle Bay, one of the most beautiful bays in the Caribbean, Mayreau is only accessible by boat.

The harbor is a favorite destination for sailboats, and sunbathing is pleasant on its arc of white sand beach bordered with palm trees. Along the coast, a few local sellers offer refreshments and souvenirs.

From the shore, the island's only road climbs to a little settlement with breathtaking views of the Tobago Cays. The majority of tourists come to Saline Bay's port. This quiet location is especially lovely for couples to visit.

7. The Canouan

Many of the greatest beaches in St. Vincent and the Grenadines may be found on Canouan, if that's what you're looking for.

This little island, located about 40 kilometers south of St. Vincent, has stunning white sand beaches and great snorkeling because of a barrier reef that shields the island's Atlantic side.

Situated along the northern half of the island, facing a well regarded golf course, are the Mandarin Oriental, Canouan and Canouan

Estate Resort & Villas, which are the preferred accommodations for most visitors to the island.

You may always hire a boat, anchor offshore, and spend the day lazing on the gorgeous beaches if you don't want to stay at one of these upscale resorts.

8. Essential

Rock stars, super-rich people, and celebrities all congregate at Exclusive Mustique. This five-kilometer private island has its own general store and airstrip, as well as exclusive private villas and The Cotton House, the only five-star hotel.

Princess Margaret, Tommy Hilfiger, Mick Jagger, and other celebrities have all visited this small piece of heaven, and some of them still own homes there.

Just offshore are coral reefs that beckon, and the island is surrounded by white sand beaches that are perfect for swimming and snorkeling. One favorite is Macaroni Beach.

Activities in Mustique also include diving, fishing, kayaking, tennis, and horseback riding throughout the island.

9. Saint Vincent's Kingstown

Kingstown is the capital and primary commercial hub of St. Vincent and the Grenadines, located on St. Vincent (Saint Vincent) island. The town has a classic Caribbean appeal, and although most visitors see it as a starting point for other islands, there are some worthwhile tourist attractions here.

The charming downtown area is enhanced by cobblestone lanes and colonial structures; if you're wondering what to do in Kingstown, St. Vincent, its elegant churches are among the highlights. St George's Cathedral, built in the Georgian style in 1820, has lovely stained-glass windows, and St Mary's Catholic Cathedral, built in the Romanesque style in 1823, has Gothic spires and columns and arches.

The oldest botanical gardens in the West Indies, St. Vincent Botanical Gardens, should not be missed by anyone with an affinity for gardening. Looking for things to do in St. Vincent while on a cruise ship? Spend a few hours strolling around lovely gardens covered with palm trees.

Fort Charlotte is perched high on a hill north of the city and offers stunning views over Kingstown and the surrounding islands.

Hiking the well-known Vermont Nature Trail, which is around 14 kilometers from Kingstown, is a great way to get in touch with nature lovers and see the rare Saint Vincent parrot.

A highly awaited Beaches resort in St. Vincent is set to open at the old Buccament Bay Resort, about a 20-minute drive north of Kingstown.

10. Estate Gardens of Montréal
It's difficult to find a more serene location than the verdant Montréal Gardens. Perched 1,500 feet above sea level, this heavenly location is said to heal your ailments. Additionally, the trip from Kingstown will take roughly an hour.

The 7.5 acres of grounds are peppered with formal rainforests and vibrant gardens that are a visual feast for the eyes and the nose. The multi-level estate is crisscrossed by a river, and well-kept walkways facilitate exploration for guests of all ages and skill levels.

Tourists are treated to breathtaking views of the Grand Bonhomme mountain, the seashore, deep rainforest, and banana plantations in the distance.

Though not as large as the St. Vincent Botanical Gardens, this site is nevertheless rather remarkable. Bring a camera; you'll want to capture the breathtaking blossoms forever.

They have been known to shut on occasion, so make sure they're open before you leave.

11. El Petit St. Vincent

The island of Petit St. Vincent is a tropical paradise. Also referred to as PSV, this privately owned island is home to the exclusive Petit St. Vincent Resort, where visitors are pampered in private villas with views of the ocean dotted throughout the bays and slopes.

The villas are devoid of TVs and phones to maintain the peace and quiet of the island. Rather, the attentive staff receives signals via colorful flags.

The resort is part of the Small Luxury Hotels of the World network and spans the whole island. It's also a popular honeymoon location and among the most upscale all-inclusive resorts in the Caribbean.

12. Island of Palm

A little slice of heaven is Palm Island. The island gets its name from the many coconut palms that the resort's previous owners planted. It is home to the Palm Island Resort & Spa, one of the greatest beach resorts in St. Vincent and the Grenadines, as well as a scattering of vacation villas.

There are five white-sand beaches along the coast, and the clear turquoise sea immediately offshore offers great snorkeling. The island is just a short boat trip from Union Island and has a tiny airport.

In addition to snorkeling, popular activities on the island include paddleboarding, kayaking, sailing, bicycling, indulging in fresh seafood at the resort's restaurants, and lounging on the stunning beaches.

13. The scenic Leeward Highway drive

A worthwhile sightseeing excursion is the Leeward Highway Scenic Drive. over the protected west coast of St. Vincent, this 40-kilometer route winds over cliff tops and picturesque coastal sections, connecting Kingstown and Richmond Beach.

Along the way are several notable tourist sites, coconut farms, black sand beaches, and indigenous settlements. A 600 AD carved face may be seen at Carib Rock along the route.

Barrouallie, a little fishing community featuring petroglyphs and a Carib stone shrine, is another popular destination for tourists. Here, the hunt for pilot whales is still a tradition.

The path comes to an end close to Richmond Beach's famous swimming hole, which has black sands. La Soufrière, the island's tallest peak and an active volcano, is seen in the distance.

Tours to the Falls of Baleine, an 18-meter waterfall near St. Vincent's northwest point, leave from this section of shore. There are no roads leading to the falls, thus the only ways to get there are by boat or on foot.

14. Union Island

Union Island, which is capped by striking volcanic peaks, serves as both the southern entrance point for St. Vincent and the Grenadines and the starting point for island-hopping excursions. It's a well-liked kitesurfing spot as well.

Ashton and Clifton are the two main communities on the island. Hikes into the hills begin in Ashton, whereas Clifton has the majority of the tourist amenities, including stores, eateries, an airport, and a marina. If you're searching for a little nightlife or are going to kitesurf, this is the place to go.

Richmond Bay and Belmont Bay, located on the island's north shore, are home to the two nicest beaches.

Caribbean Islands close to St. Vincent and the Grenadines: Union Island is the starting point for ferries to Carriacou, one of Grenada's most popular tourist destinations. Because of the aromatic nutmeg, cinnamon, and other spices that flourish in its rich soil, this picturesque location is referred to as "the Spice Island". These two locations, together with St. Lucia, which is located farther north, provide lush landscape and a true Caribbean experience. Some of the most opulent all-inclusive resorts in the Caribbean can be found in both of these places.

Historical Landmarks

Historical landmarks in St. Vincent are locations or structures that are significant to the nation and its people historically or culturally. The history of St. Vincent is influenced by several times and events, including the Carib resistance, European colonialism, African enslavement and emancipation, and the independence struggle. These are all reflected in them. They also highlight the island's varied and stunning natural features, such the bays, waterfalls, tropical woods, and volcanic mountains. You may discover more about St.

Vincent and its people's history, present, and future by going to these historical sites.

1. La Soufrière Volcano Hiking

Visitors to the crater of La Soufriere, a volcano rising 1,234 meters above sea level, may experience this well-liked guided climb. This mountain, which is still active, is the highest in St. Vincent. In 1979, it last erupted. On the leeward path, the trek takes six to eight hours total, whereas on the windward trail, it takes three to four hours. Along the route, hikers may learn about the local flora and fauna, cloud and rain forests, and other locations. At the summit of the ascent, they may also investigate the crater.

2. The Churches of St. Kingstown

Visitors may witness colonial houses, cobblestone lanes, and the 1820s

Georgian-style cathedral St. George's Anglican Cathedral in Kingstown, the state capital. The building has windows with stained glass. Built in the Romanesque architectural style in 1823, St. Mary's Catholic Cathedral has Gothic spires, columns, and arches.

3. Fort Charlotte

Perched atop a hill with a commanding view of Kingstown Harbor, this fort dates back to the British colonial period. Located on the leeward side of the island at an elevation of 601 feet above sea level, the fort is the principal early 19th-century structure on St. Vincent. From the fort, you can see the island of Bequia, Young Island, Kingstown, and the Caribbean Sea. On clear days, Grenada may be seen from around 90 miles south.

4. Vermont Nature Trail

Hikers on this walk will see a lush rainforest with a diverse range of tropical flora and unique views. The St. Vincent Parrot Reserve offers particularly wonderful sightings of the St. Vincent Parrot in its native environment. Nature enthusiasts should not miss this walk because of its abundance of tropical vegetation, stunning views of the cliffs and valleys, and both.

5. Botanical Gardens of St. Vincent

These gardens were created in 1765 and are the oldest in the West Indies. The roughly 20-acre gardens are home to both native and exotic plants and trees, such as hibiscus, cinnamon, nutmeg, mahogany, palms, and a breadfruit tree that is said to have been developed from a seedling that the renowned Captain Bligh of "Mutiny on the Bounty" brought to the island.

Views of the St. Vincent parrot are given at the onsite aviary.

6. Old Hegg Turtle Sanctuary

Orton "Brother" King established this sea turtle hatchery in 1995 and has been breeding turtles from eggs ever since, hoping to boost the survival rates of these increasingly endangered creatures. King was the only survivor of a shipwreck off the coast of Martinique, which gave him the idea to create the hatchery. A guy who spotted him assumed he was a turtle when he washed ashore on the beach. King, having been rescued, vowed that while he was out in the wide water, turtles had shielded him from sharks. This made him want to defend the turtles that had come to his rescue.

7. Dark View Falls

Situated at the base of La Soufrière Volcano, the falls cascade from a Richmond River branch, one above the other, down a steep cliff and into a deep natural pool at the bottom. A natural bamboo bridge is crossed by the route leading to the falls after passing through a bamboo forest. A terrific adventurous climb, and the pools give excellent possibilities for refreshing dips.

8. The Owia Salt Pond

situated close to the Owia settlement on the island's northeastern shore. The Black Caribs, the indigenous people of St. Vincent, live in this region. Lava from the Soufriere volcano formed the pond as it cooled and reached the sea. Waves breaking over the rocks replenish the pond. The mild saline water of the location is a favorite bathing spot among visitors, since it is believed to provide health advantages. Well-maintained grounds with a gazebo, fire pits, showers, tables, and seats around the pond.

9. Fort Duvernette

Atop a volcanic rock off the coast of Villa sits this fort. An unsettling fort constructed to protect Calliaqua village. It provides a full 360-degree view of the southern side of the island. Slabbed into the rock is a 225-step spiral staircase that leads to the fort, which is located 200 feet above sea level. A picnic area and two gun batteries are also present at the location. Only a boat can get to it.

10. Wallilabou Anchorage

Wallilabou Anchorage, well-known for its historical value and natural beauty, used as a shooting site for the "Pirates of the Caribbean" film. There are relics from abandoned movie sets on display, providing insight into the island's history with the motion picture business.

11. St. Mary's Cathedral

One of the oldest cathedrals in the Caribbean is St. Mary's Cathedral, also referred to as the Cathedral of the Assumption. It is a significant cultural and historical landmark that was constructed in the middle of the 19th century and has Gothic Revival architecture.

12. Black Point Tunnel

A historic railroad tunnel from the 19th century, the Black Point Tunnel is sometimes referred to as the Richmond Vale Railway Tunnel. It was a component of the sugar industry's transportation network.

13. Fort Granby

Fort Granby was built in the eighteenth century to act as a defensive stronghold against any intruders. Visitors may now examine the fort's remains and understand its historical importance.

14. Petroglyphs of Yambou

Ancient rock carvings known as the Yambou Petroglyphs include a variety of symbols and characters. A glimpse of the native Carib culture that once flourished on the island may be seen in these petroglyphs.

These St. Vincent historical monuments, which range from colonial forts to cultural and natural heritage sites, highlight the island's rich past. Discovering these sites provides an intriguing historical voyage on this treasure of the Caribbean.

Outdoor Activities and Adventure

St. Vincent provides both thrill-seekers and nature lovers with an abundance of outdoor sports and experiences due to its immaculate shoreline and verdant terrain. Here is a carefully chosen list of things to do while discovering this Caribbean treasure's natural wonders:

1. Mount Soufrière Volcano hiking

The highest point on St. Vincent and an active volcano, La Soufrière, is a must-hike if you're searching for an exhilarating and unforgettable experience. Hikers with a moderate level of fitness may complete the four-hour trek in one go. You may hire a guide or sign up for a group trip at the Rabacca Trailhead, where you will begin your journey. The walk will lead you through verdant rainforests where you may take in the clean air and the sounds of nature while seeing unusual birds and flora. As you ascend farther, you will see that the surrounding area turns from green to black as you approach the volcanic zone. The sight of the enormous crater, which is filled with a turquoise lake, as well as the expansive views of the island and the sea from the summit will astound you. Additionally, you will get to see the volcano's distinctive geological characteristics, such lava domes, fumaroles, and sulfur deposits. A once-in-a-lifetime experience that will leave you breathless and ecstatic is hiking La Soufrière.

2. Tobago Cays Snorkeling and Diving

Snorkeling or diving in the crystal-clear waters of the Tobago Cays Marine Park is one of the most breathtaking ways to take in its splendor. A reef formed like a horseshoe surrounds the collection of five tiny, deserted islands known as the Tobago Cays. The coral reefs are teeming with vibrant fish, turtles, rays, and other marine life, and the water is so pure that you can see the bottom from the top. You may snorkel or dive at several spots surrounding the cays, such as the Baradal Turtle Sanctuary, where you can swim with the peaceful green turtles, or the Mayreau Gardens, where you can view the spectacular coral formations. For those with an affinity for the undersea world, diving and snorkeling in the Tobago Cays Marine Park are a must-do experience.

3. Take a Grenadine cruise

Sailing the Grenadine Islands is the ultimate Caribbean vacation. The Grenadines are a group of thirty-two islands and cays extending from Grenada to St. Vincent. You may select from a range of sailing alternatives, such as a hired yacht, a catamaran, or a sailboat, depending on your budget and desire. You may sail the islands at your own speed and find secret treasures that are not reachable by land. You may anchor at the quaint island of Bequia, where you can take in the local customs and food, or you can visit the well-known Tobago Cays, where you can go snorkeling with turtles and rays. Additionally, you may unwind on Palm Island's immaculate beaches or take in St. Lucia's breathtaking views of the Pitons. The Grenadines are a sailing haven for novices and pros alike because of their placid seas and consistent breezes. Sailing the Grenadines is a fantastic opportunity to enjoy the variety and beauty of the Caribbean.

4. Indian Bay Kayaking

Kayaking on the calm waters of Indian Bay is a great way to spend time outside and enjoy the scenery. Surrounded by exotic vegetation and luxuriant foliage, Indian Bay is a stunning bay. You can paddle along the bay while taking in the sights of the hills and shore by renting a kayak or signing up for a guided trip. Some of the bay's aquatic inhabitants, including fish, turtles, dolphins, and possibly whales, may be seen throughout the route. In addition to being enjoyable and physically active, kayaking in Indian Bay is a fantastic opportunity to take in the island's natural beauty and variety.

5. Hike to Dark View Falls

Try trekking to one of St. Vincent's most breathtaking waterfalls, Dark View Falls, for an exciting and unforgettable experience. This trek is appropriate for all levels of fitness and takes 15 to 20 minutes. You may purchase your ticket and get some refreshments in the welcome center, where you will begin your journey. You may soak in the shade and the sounds of nature as you walk through a beautiful tropical jungle. To increase the pleasure and excitement, you may choose to cross the Richmond River by a traditional bridge or a bamboo bridge. Next, you'll come to a clearing in the center of a bamboo forest, where the first waterfall—roughly a hundred feet high—can be seen. You may swim in the naturally formed pool below the falls or ascend to the about 200-foot-high second cascade. The second waterfall has a breathtaking view of the valley and is more private. A wonderful approach to see St. Vincent's natural variety and beauty is to hike to Dark View Falls. It's also a nice way to unwind and cool down.

6. Tubing along the Buccament Valley River

River tubing at Buccament Valley is a fantastic pastime that provides an exciting and enjoyable way to see St. Vincent's gorgeous rainforest. Sailing down the Buccament River, which meanders through the picturesque valley of the St. Vincent Parrot Reserve, you will get into a huge inflatable tube. In addition to the serene areas where you may unwind and take in the breathtaking views of the tropical flora and wildlife, you will experience the exhilaration of negotiating the mild rapids that add excitement to your journey. The nation's official bird, the rare and beautiful St. Vincent Parrot, may even be seen to you as it soars above the forest canopy. Buccament Valley river tubing is a fantastic opportunity to combine adventure and the breathtaking scenery of St. Vincent into one amazing activity.

7. A Visit to the Owia Salt Ponds

Situated on the extreme northeastern shore of the island of St. Vincent, the Owia Salt Ponds are one of the most breathtaking sights to see. These naturally occurring saltwater lakes were created thousands of years ago when lava from the Soufriere Volcano cooled and joined the ocean. Surrounded by volcanic rocks, the pools provide a peaceful haven for swimming and snorkeling while shielding them from the surf. In addition to soaking in the breath-blowing vistas of the Atlantic Ocean and the verdant slopes, you may enjoy the warm water and the vibrant fish. For travelers of all ages, the Owia Salt Ponds are a hidden treasure that provide a unique and fascinating experience.

8. Birdwatching on the Vermont Nature Trail

One of the greatest places in St. Vincent2 for birding is the Vermont Nature Trail, which you would love to explore if you are an enthusiast of birds. The 4-kilometer walk winds through a verdant jungle where you may see more than 50 different kinds of birds2. You'll pass by a variety of flora, including fruits, flowers, and plants, and you'll get beautiful views of the nearby valleys and mountains. The trail's high point is the opportunity to see the St. Vincent Parrot, the island's sole endangered and colorful bird of state1. Anyone interested in seeing the splendor and variety of St. Vincent's birds must visit the Vermont Nature Trail.

The island of St. Vincent has something to offer everyone. St. Vincent offers a wide variety of outdoor activities that highlight the island's natural beauty and cultural diversity, whether you're looking for peaceful excursions or heart-pounding experiences. Hiking to the top of an active volcano, swimming in a salt pond, diving into vibrant coral reefs, and sailing to neighboring islands are all options. In addition, you may take pleasure in the food, culture, and animals of this paradise in the Caribbean. You will be astounded by the sights, sounds, and experiences of St. Vincent, regardless of what you decide to do. You will have wonderful recollections from this island and a strong desire to go back.

Local Markets and Shopping

While St. Vincent and the Grenadines may not be the best place to buy, those seeking genuine mementos can discover a number of quaint businesses and interesting crafts at neighborhood markets.

Basil's Bazaar
Situated next to the well-known bar itself, Basil's Bazaar is a little store where you can get anything from straw hats and candles to t-shirts and elegant resort attire. Everyone will undoubtedly know where you've been since "Basil's Mustique" is emblazoned on most items in one way or another, but isn't that the whole idea?

Sargeant Brothers Model Boat Shop
Bequia has been home to the boat-building industry since the 1800s. Since it produced the biggest wooden boat in the area, the island was

once referred to as the "boat-building capital of the West Indies." Though production has slowed down over time, building is still going on, but on a much smaller scale. Locations such as Sargeant Brothers Model Boat Shop, located near the Port Elizabeth ferry landing, are where Benson Phillips and other artisans create and market their models.

Their boats are extraordinarily realistic and intricate, having been handcrafted using carving knives, chisels, and hand planes. Pick from a variety of boats, including motor boats, sailboats, whale boats, and wooden schooners, or have Phillips create a personalized model of your dream vessel.

A few boats are always available for immediate purchase; the most basic versions take approximately a week to build. Prices range from roughly $250 to $7,000.

Nzimbu Browne

St. Vincent isn't particularly known for its shopping, but if you're looking for the ideal memento, Nzimbu Browne's well-known banana artwork is a great choice. In addition to tourism, St. Vincent's economy is mostly fueled by banana cultivation.

Browne makes environmentally friendly artwork with a strong feeling of location by using the waste products of the business, banana leaves. His paintings include local landscapes that are enriched with fragments of colorful, dried leaves.

He also creates tie-dyed clothes and goatskin drums, if you're not into art. Although McKie's Hill in Kingstown serves as his studio, he often sets up shop in front of the Cobblestone Inn on Upper Bay Street.

Pink House Mustique

Though the little town center of Mustique has a few stores, you should definitely pay attention to the two pastel cottages with gingerbread trim. Pink House specializes in sophisticated, hand-painted silk kaftans and sarongs by local designer Lotty B. It also sells dinnerware, jewelry, and accessories, as well as beach and resort clothing for men, women, and children. Purple House next door has less priced beachwear, kid's toys, jewelry, souvenirs, and kaftans.

St. Vincent Botanical Gardens Gift Shop

There's a really good gift store within the St. Vincent Botanical Gardens in Kingstown, with everything from locally created artwork, crafts, and ceramics to literature on the island, children's toys, genuine souvenirs, refreshments, and refreshing beverages.

Naturally, the gift store is decked with plants, and it also has island-inspired carnival costumes.

St. Vincent Craftsmen's Centre

The Craftsman's Centre is located on Frenchs St., three blocks inland from the shore. It offers fairly priced, locally manufactured products such as colorful batik fabric, hand-painted calabashes, beautiful grass mats in sizes ranging from place mats to entire floor mats, and more. Only cash! (P.S. To transport home, the grass mats fold or roll into a tidy bundle.)

St. Vincent Cruise Ship Terminal Shops

There are over twenty shops, restaurants, and boutiques at the Kingstown cruise ship port, most of which serve passengers but are open to all customers. Along with the usual duty-free merchandise, you may purchase locally produced hot sauces, spices, soaps, lotions, jewelry crafted from seeds and shells, and other handicrafts. Just be aware that some stores are only open during ship ports.

CHAPTER 5. Island Hopping in the Grenadines

Overview of Grenadine Islands

The Grenadine Islands are a group of over 600 islands and islets in the Caribbean Sea that are located in the Lesser Antilles' southeast. They are split between the two nations and are located between the bigger islands of Saint Vincent and Grenada. While the southern Grenadines are a part of Grenada, the northern Grenadines are part of Saint Vincent and the Grenadines.

The Grenadines have a tropical environment with mild temperatures and moderate rainfall, and they are mostly volcanic in nature. Their aquatic life, coral reefs, and unspoiled beauty are well-known. Several of the islands, including Bequia, Mustique, Canouan, and Palm Island, are well-liked travel destinations. Others, including Calivigny, Petit Nevis, and Petit Mustique, are privately held or deserted.

The Caribs lived on the Grenadines and utilized them for fishing and food collection, however their history is not widely known. In 1650, the Caribs and the British resisted the French claim to Grenada and the Grenadines. Before the British took over in 1762, the islands had several owners. Grenada and St Vincent split the Grenadines in 1791, and in 1974 and 1979, the two countries gained independence.

Choosing Your st Vincent's Island Itinerary

A 3 Days Itinerary

If you are considering a trip to this stunning location, you might want to consider creating a 3-day itinerary that will give you a taste of the various activities, cultures, and landscapes the islands have to offer. You can discover the breathtaking beaches and coral reefs, the densely forested volcanic mountains, the rich history and legacy, and the energetic local way of life. Whatever your preferences, St. Vincent and the Grenadines has plenty to offer, whether you're searching for adventure, relaxation, or cultural immersion.

Day 1: Historical Sites and Kingstown Exploration Morning

Breakfast in Kingstown: At one of the town's cafes, begin your day with a hearty local meal.

Investigate Heritage Square: Go around Heritage Square and its environs. Explore historical landmarks such as St. Mary's Cathedral and the Cobblestone Inn.

In the afternoon

Lunch at a Local Spot: In Kingstown, have some regional Vincentian food for lunch.

Botanic Gardens: Spend the afternoon at St. Vincent and the Grenadines Botanic Gardens, one of the oldest in the Western Hemisphere. Explore the diverse plant life and the Nicholas Wildlife Aviary.

Evening

supper in Kingstown: Enjoy supper at a local restaurant in Kingstown.

Nightlife: If you're up for it, experience the local nightlife with some live music or a calm evening at a waterfront pub.

Day 2: La Soufrière Volcano and Beach Relaxation Morning

climb La Soufrière: Begin your day early with a climb to the peak of La Soufrière. Witness the amazing views from the summit and experience the unique volcanic terrain.

In the afternoon

Lunch at Owia Salt Ponds: Head to the northeastern shore for lunch at Owia Salt Ponds. Enjoy local cuisine and a dip in the natural pools.

Beach Time at Vermont Beach: Spend the day at Vermont Beach, a calm place with golden beaches and blue waves.

Evening

Sunset at Fort Duvernette: Head to Fort Duvernette for panoramic vistas and a magnificent sunset.

supper in Bequia: Take a boat to Bequia for supper, visiting this picturesque island in the evening.

Day 3: Island Hopping in the Grenadines
Morning

Breakfast in Bequia: Enjoy breakfast at a beach café in Bequia.

Boat to Mustique: Take a boat to Mustique, noted for its opulent environment and stunning beaches.

In the afternoon
Discover Mustique: Take an afternoon to discover Mustique. Take a walk down Macaroni Beach, stop at the well-known Basil's Bar, and take in the upscale atmosphere.

Lunch in Mustique: Enjoy a midday meal at one of the posh restaurants on Mustique.

Evening

Returned to St. Vincent: Return to St. Vincent via nighttime boat.

Have a goodbye supper at a restaurant by the sea while reflecting on your brief but unforgettable visit.

This program offers a well-balanced combination of island hopping experiences, recreational activities, and cultural discovery. Tailor it to your tastes and the particular celebrations or events taking place while you're there. Always be on the lookout for any travel warnings or adjustments to the hours of operation of restaurants and attractions.

A 5 Days Itinerary

First Day

First stop: Kingstown

You will have to wait until after midday to check in after an early morning flight. A terrific option to spend your (nearly) whole day on the main island of St. Vincent is to visit Kingstown.

The capital city may not appear to provide much to do at first glance. But don't fall for it. Stay and enjoy the island's original culture.

Take a stroll along the main avenue to see this historic port city's distinct atmosphere. Take in the intricate intricacies of the various buildings' colonial-style architecture. Observe the street sellers offering a wide variety of items from their vehicle trunks and on the pavement. As the air fills with informal chats, listen to the distinctive twang of the Vincentian dialect. Anybody who looks at you should smile. And if you notice anything that piques your attention, help out a few street vendors.

Get meals and beverages at The Cobblestone Inn when you need a break from the heat and from strolling. Living true to its name, this little hotel and restaurant provides the ideal escape from the bustle of the city. Order a meal from the extensive menu and ask the friendly bartender to create you the ideal rum punch. Until you're ready to leave the city, unwind in the eating area outside.

The best kind of transportation is the minibus, which is widely accessible. Be prepared for a cramped journey since they are professionals at cramming too many passengers into these little cars.

The one-way cost of the minibus travel is EC $5.

The estimated price of lunch is EC $50.

Stop 2: Duvernette Fort

Take a water taxi to Fort Duvernette from Villa Beach as the sun sets and the temperature begins to dip. This ancient landmark, also called Rock Fort, is perched 195 feet above sea level atop a tall, narrow rock that protrudes abruptly out of the water. You must ascend the steps that follow the contour of the rock face in order to reach the summit. You may wish to avoid this sport if you are afraid of heights since they are rather steep. But the ascent is worthwhile because of the breathtaking sights.

Though the views from the summit are amazing, be aware that, at least during my visit, heavy plants obscure certain vistas. Therefore, even if it's still a beautiful sight, be prepared for some obstruction to what should be a 360-degree vista.

Water taxi is the only form of transportation.

Water taxi fare: 15 EC (about five minutes).

Free admission to the fort

Bring water to drink, comfortable shoes, and a strong heart as you stroll.

Day Two

All Day: Drive to Owia Salt Pond
A fantastic place to go on a road trip is Owia Salt Pond, a natural feature located in the island's north. Locals often go there to jump

from the rocks into the choppy waves outside the pond. However, it also attracts visitors who like relaxing in the safe and calm saltwater pools for a swim.

This destination may be visited on a tour, however if you want to go alone, I suggest hiring a vehicle for the day. Although there are some rough and uneven spots on the route, it is generally straightforward to navigate. And there will be a ton of breathtaking vistas that will cause you to stop and take in the beauty.

Prepare yourself as you must descend several hundred steps to reach the beach.and climb the identical stairs to exit. But when you get to the pond, you'll be treated to an amazing sight. Envision this: the massive ocean waves' white foam as they crash into the dark rocks. Tall mountains clad in verdant foliage. The still water of the salt pond in front. The blue sky provided the ideal backdrop. You'll always treasure this Mother Nature scene.

One could easily spend an hour or two here relaxing and taking tons of Instagram-worthy photos, whether they want to go on an adventure or just hang out in the shallow water and make friends with the fish that swim around them.

Transportation method: Hired Automobile

Rental fee: $75 USD

$10 EC is the entrance fee to Salt Pond.

Day Three

All day, Bequia

Pack a beach bag, board the boat, and get ready for an exciting day of beach hopping in Bequia after a peaceful night. Clear water and verdant vegetation abound on Bequia, the second largest island in the Grenadines. Adorable eateries around the promenade provide breathtaking views of the azure ocean. And when you imagine the ideal Caribbean holiday, the well-known Princess Margaret Beach with its white sand is even more gorgeous than you could have imagined.

It's important to keep in mind that a lot of Bequia businesses shut from August through the beginning of October, which is considered the off-season. The single restaurant at the beach is closed, so make plans in advance and eat before you go.

Our Bequia day was nearly wonderful, but it got off to a rough start since we weren't sure what to do. We thus hope you may benefit from our errors. Consider the differences between what we did and what we ought to have done.

What took place was:
- traveled straight to the beach in a minibus, requiring us to descend a lengthy and uneven slope to reach the water's edge.
- When I arrived at the beach, I discovered that the one restaurant there was closed.
- After approximately twenty-five minutes of walking down a damaged and cracked route by the lake, through a forest, and past a shuttered hotel, we arrived at a boardwalk with numerous open restaurants.

- As a reward for our labors, we had some food and beverages before hiring a boat to return to the beach for a mere US $20.
- Later that day, the same boat took us to the port.

What you ought to do is

- Pick a spot for breakfast or an early lunch as you stroll down the promenade away from the dock. It won't be more than five minutes away.
- To get you through the remainder of the day, get some food and beverages.
- You may spend the whole day playing in the sea at Princess Margaret Beach if you rent a boat.
- To ensure you arrive in time for the 4 pm ferry departure, arrange for the same boat to pick you up at 3:40 pm.

Ferry service is one way to get to Bequia.

Times of departure: 4 PM (from Bequia) and 8 AM (from Kingstown).

The round-trip ferry fare is $50 EC.

Water taxi is Bequia's mode of transportation.

$30 USD for a one-way taxi ride

Lunch is expected to cost EC $75 (drinks included).

Rent a beach chair for EC $25.

Day Four

Drive west of St. Vincent for the whole day.

You have one last chance to hire a vehicle and explore, heading west, on your final full day on the island. Driving up to the Wallilabou

Waterfalls, which I had heard so much about, was our first objective. All I had planned was a short stroll and some time to relax in and around the plunge pool, but

Stop 1: The Waterfalls of Wallilabou
This was an instance of high expectations not being met by reality. The waterfall was rather simple and extremely "small."A little pool, barely big enough to accommodate three people at a time, was filled with water from two small streams. It was a little underwhelming, to say the least, for someone who loves waterfalls like myself.

Fortunately, the falls are surrounded by a verdant garden with gorgeous flowers and lively bright green lizards who like to scamper about you and even inside your luggage if you let them. Although our expectations for a spectacular encounter were not met, this stop was nevertheless a pleasant location to stop and relax after all the travel, snap some beautiful photos, and maybe have a modest lunch if I return.

Second Stop: Caribbean Museum's Pirates

The Pirates of the Caribbean Museum was conveniently located a short distance from Wallilabou, which was a bonus for seeing the falls! The series was shot in SVG for a number of its films, and this museum houses much of the set. A groundskeeper-led tour is available for "as much as you can afford."

Even yet, don't anticipate ornate displays and costly props when you visit. In addition to the area's natural splendor, the museum is a very interesting spot in a haphazard, eccentric kind of manner. Roughly nailed to boards on the walls are screenplay pages and photos from a few of the shootings. On the ground, in a kind of exhibit, are film canisters and reels. In the courtyard remains the hangman's noose. You may even stroll along the same jetty that Captain Jack Sparrow used to walk upon before his ship sank under the sea.

Buccament Bay Beach Resort is stop three.

While returning, take a little diversion to the empty Buccament Bay Resort. Once a vast and magnificent all-inclusive resort, it's now a deserted village with abandoned bungalows and vacant pools. Even if the enclosure is depressing, the beachfront portion of the land is still public and well-kept.

Expense: Nothing

Fourth Stop: Fort Charlotte

Fort Charlotte is a great place to make your last road trip stop. The Fort, which was constructed by the British in 1806, sits 600 feet above Kingstown and offers breathtaking views over the island's leeward side. Built to fend against French attacks, Carib disturbances, and slave uprisings, the fort was once staffed by 600 troops and equipped with 34 cannons pointing both inland and toward the coast. Several decades later, it serves as a poignant reminder of the Caribbean's convoluted history and is the ideal location for anybody seeking an aerial perspective of Kingstown and its environs.

Expense: Nothing

Day Five

Airport, Late Lunch, and Hotel QT Time

We could enjoy a substantial portion of the day since we had scheduled a PM return flight. Still, we were unwilling to risk our time. You shouldn't either. That's why I recommend making the most of your last day to make advantage of your hotel's amenities. Enjoy a leisurely morning. Relax beside the swimming area. After that, have a delicious meal and some beverages. If you would like, take a nap. Next, wrap up your packing and give your cab a call.

You only have five days to enjoy yourself, so you don't want to squander time or cash. I hope some of the advice in this itinerary for St. Vincent and the Grenadines may come in use when you arrange your own vacation to beautiful SVG. Each experience I've shared was distinct in its own right.

A 7 Days Itinerary

Day 1: Itinerary for the St. Vincent Cruise

Blue Lagoon / Mustique

At Blue Lagoon Marina in Ratho Mill, St. Vincent, you may begin your sailing schedule for the week by checking in, loading and stocking your boat, and making sure you have everything you need. An IGA store is located nearby where you may get supplies for your journey.

You may start traveling to Mustique, which is around two hours distant from Blue Lagoon.

Mustique

Mustique is a private island that was purchased by Lord Glenconner in 1958 with the intention of serving as a haven for affluent individuals. The Mustique Company, which is controlled by those who own real estate and land on this tropical paradise, now owns and operates the island.

The Mustique Company provides a variety of activities on the island, including hiking, water sports, tennis, yoga, and spa services. View their whole selection of products online. Mustique has stunning white sand beaches that are ideal for lounging in the sun.

Suggested Dining Establishments and Events:

- Mustique, St. Vincent and the Grenadines: Basil's Bar
- Mustique, St. Vincent and the Grenadines' Firefly Restaurant & Hotel

Day 2: Tobago Cays/Musique

You will sail to Tobago Cays for the second stop on our sailing journey through St. Vincent. This location is well known for having one of the most exquisite anchorages. Tobago Cay, with its amazing horseshoe reef, is the ideal place to go snorkeling. Go underwater to interact with sea turtles, or come up to the surface to interact with the island's resident iguanas and tortoises.

Five tiny islands and coral reefs make up Tobago Cays. All of them are deserted and part of the Tobago Cays Marine, an amazing location to visit on our St. Vincent sailing trip that aids in maintaining, safeguarding, and managing the amazing environment found in the cays' pristine seas.

Suggested Dining Establishments and Events:

- Tobago Cays, Mayreau Gardens Reef, St. Vincent and the Grenadines
- Purunia Shipwreck, Tobago Cays, St. Vincent and the Grenadines, Mayreau Western Coast

Day 3: Tobago Cays

Day 3 of our St. Vincent sailing itinerary is also devoted to Tobago Cays. You should make the most of your time in the Southern Grenadines, which is known as the "Jewel in the Crown." There are lots of things to do on land at Tobago Cays in addition to the incredible activities that await you below the water's surface. Spend the day taking in the sun and discovering these stunning Cays via hiking, bird viewing, and sunbathing.

Suggested Dining Establishments and Events:

- Observe seabird nesting from your boat at the Catholic Rock Bird Sanctuary in Tobago Cays, St. Vincent and the Grenadines.
- St. Vincent and the Grenadines: Petit Bateau, James Bay, Petit Rameau, hiking

Day 4: Petit St. Vincent / Tobago Cays

It's time to depart Tobago Cays and go to Petit St. Vincent after a few days. Here, you may set up on Mopion, a little sand islet, where there's a little canopy made of coconut thatch to provide some shade. Numerous guests will engrave their names and initials on the umbrella's post.

There are plenty of things to do on Petit St. Vincent, since the whole island operates like an opulent resort. During our sailing cruise in St. Vincent, spend your time windsurfing, snorkeling, scuba diving, and grilling on the beach while listening to steel pan music.

Suggested Dining Establishments and Events:

- Golf Course: 18-hole/9-hole, located in the Petit St. Vincent Resort in Petit St. Vincent
- Petit St. Vincent Resort, Petit St. Vincent, Pavilion Restaurant

Day 5: Chatham Bay / Petit St. Vincent

You may unwind and unwind by sailing to Chatham Bay on Union Island, the next island in our St. Vincent sailing trip. Visitors may enjoy the vast golden sand beach at Chatham Bay in addition to the kayaking, snorkeling, and diving opportunities available. An island of seclusion, let yourself unwind and take in the day's vibe.

But at night, Seckie and Vanessa's beach restaurant in Chatham Bay provides lively entertainment, and you may conclude the evening dancing in the sand. You may quickly go to Clifton, Union Island's major port, if you're in the mood for even more activity.

Suggested Dining Establishments and Events:

- Aqua Restaurant, Chatham Bay, Union Island, St. Vincent and the Grenadines.

Day 6: Mayreau/Chatham Bay

Since there are no official roads in Mayreau, hiking is the ideal way to pass the time. The greatest climb will get you to the top of the hill, where the church offers breathtaking views. This hike, which takes around one hour, is a fantastic excursion on our sailing route to St. Vincent.

There are around 400 people living in Mayreau, the smallest of the Grenadines. On our St. Vincent sailing route, Mayreau—sometimes known as "the island time forgot"—is a perfect place to disconnect from the outside world.

Suggested Dining Establishments and Events:

- Mayreau, St. Vincent and the Grenadines / Dennis's Hideaway

Day 7: Bequia / Mayreau

After roughly four hours at sea, you will arrive in Bequia, the last destination on our St. Vincent sailing trip, where there is enough to do. Being one of the bigger Grenadines, there are many eateries and bars here along with various beachside activities. Enjoy the beautiful town of Port Elizabeth here. Alternatively, you might choose for a guided trip of the island or hike any of the several routes that culminate in a breathtaking vista at the summit. The name Bequia, which translates to "island in the clouds," is not by accident; our St. Vincent sailing tour takes you there.

Your St. Vincent sailing trip will come to a conclusion when you sail back to Kingston after spending the day at Bequia.

Suggested Dining Establishments and Events:

- Port Elizabeth, Bequia, Bequia Maritime Museum, St. Vincent and the Grenadines
- Restaurant Firefly Bequia Plantation, Bequia, Saint Vincent and the Grenadines

Transportation Between Islands

The Grenadines Islands may be reached in a variety of methods, based on your preferences, budget, and goal. These are a few of the choices:

Fast Ferry: Between St. Vincent and the Grenadine Islands of Bequia, Canouan, and Union Island, there is passenger service provided by the jet-propelled, twin-hulled Jaden Sun high-speed vessel. Travel time to Union Island is 120 minutes, Canouan is 90 minutes, and Bequia is 30 minutes. The boat has comfortable seating, a café, and restrooms in addition to complete air conditioning.

Water Taxi: It takes around 45 minutes to get from Canouan to Union Island and 10 minutes to travel from Union Island to Mayreau. Bequia also offers regular water taxi service to and from various locations on the island, departing from the Frangipani docks. Although they might be more costly than ferries, water taxis are versatile and handy.

Plane: St. Vincent, Bequia, Canouan, Union Island, and Mustique all have airports, so you may travel between the islands as well. The flight time is roughly 45 minutes from St. Lucia to the Grenadines, and about an hour from St. Vincent to the Grenadines. The quickest and most comfortable mode of transportation is flying, but it's also the most expensive.

Unique Experiences on Each Island

Travelers may enjoy a range of activities in St. Vincent and The Grenadines, including hiking, nature trails, excursions to several stunning, unspoiled locations, diving, beaches, and, if time allows, a trip to the nearby Grenadine islands. For those who are not as daring, the capital city of Kingstown, with its well-known Botanic Gardens and other historical sites like Ft. Charlotte, provides an opportunity for visitors to gain a bird's eye perspective of the island's past while also enjoying the shopping.

St. Vincent: The biggest and most populous island in the West Indies, St. Vincent is home to Kingstown, the capital, where you can stroll among colonial buildings and cobblestone alleys and see the oldest botanical gardens in the region. Hikers can also ascend La Soufrière, an active volcano that provides breathtaking views of the island and the ocean.

Bequia: The second-biggest island, Bequia is renowned for its amiable residents and easygoing charm. You can witness the rehabilitation and release of endangered hawksbill turtles into the wild by going to the Old Hegg Turtle Sanctuary. You can also take in the vibrant Port Elizabeth waterfront and sandy beaches like Princess Margaret Beach and Lower Bay.

Mustique: The wealthy and famous frequent this private island, which is owned by the Mustique Company, because of its opulent villas, upscale resorts, and quiet beaches. Additionally, you can check out the Cotton House, a former plantation home converted into a boutique hotel, and Basil's Bar, a well-liked hangout for royalty and celebrities.

Canouan: A sizable resort situated on a small island, Canouan is home to the Mandarin Oriental, a five-star establishment featuring fine dining, golf, and spa services. Explore the island's natural features as well, like the turtle sanctuary, Mount Royal, the highest point, and the coral reefs.

Mayreau: With just one village and one road, Mayreau is the smallest inhabited island and is a peaceful paradise. Saline Bay and Salt Whistle Bay are two of the immaculate beaches where you can unwind while taking in the views of the Tobago Cays from the church perched on a hilltop.

Union Island: Serving as the southern entry point to the Grenadines, Union Island is a bustling center for sailors, kite surfers, and boaters. You can go to Happy Island, an artificial island constructed out of conch shells, and the lively town of Clifton, which has stores, eateries, and bars. You can also take a boat trip to the nearby islands of Palm Island and Petit St. Vincent.

Palm Island: A romantic getaway for couples and honeymooners, Palm Island is a private island resort. You may enjoy the all-inclusive facilities, such as the spa, the pool, and the beachfront bungalows, and the activities, such as kayaking, snorkeling, and sailing.

Petit St. Vincent: Another private island resort, Petit St. Vincent is a quiet retreat for people who desire serenity and seclusion. You may stay in one of the 22 cottages, each with its own flag system to indicate your requirements, and enjoy the services, such as the yoga pavilion, the spa center, and the beach bar.

Tobago Cays: The crown gem of the Grenadines, the Tobago Cays are five tiny, deserted islands that are part of a marine park. You may swim, snorkel, and dive in the crystal-clear waters, and witness the rich marine life, such as sea turtles, stingrays, and reef fish. You may also relax on the white-sand beaches, and observe the breathtaking beauty of the islands and the water.

Each island offers its own particular flavor to the collective appeal of St. Vincent and the Grenadines. Whether you desire adventure, leisure, or cultural discovery, these islands provide a broad choice of activities for any sort of tourist.

CHAPTER 6. Beaches and Water Activities

Top Beaches in St. Vincent and the Grenadines

St Vincent, the lush, untouched mainland of St Vincent and the Grenadines, is home to some stunningly magnificent beaches. The beaches of St. Vincent are still among the best-kept secrets in the Caribbean, providing a respite from the congestion of popular tourist spots.

Because of the island's volcanic beginnings, several of St. Vincent's beaches are unique among Caribbean islands in that they have gorgeous black sand. Now without further ado, let's discover St. Vincent's top beaches!

1. Questelles Beach

A local favorite, Questelles Beach is renowned for its vibrant, small-town atmosphere in addition to its breathtakingly gorgeous coastline.

This place seems more genuine since you won't often find any tourists or cruise ship passengers here. The people at the beach extend a warm greeting to you, and there is a little settlement nearby. This beach combines convenience and charm, with easy access and a modest parking lot.

At Questelle's Beach, the ocean is very serene and the sand has a golden hue. A little beach bar emits the sound of enjoyable music, creating the ideal ambiance for unwinding and enjoying the sun.

Some kids on the beach informed us that you can climb the hill to view the wreckage, which is sitting on a rock just out of sight. We didn't use them for the expedition since we were without shoes, but I think you might see it if you go snorkeling far enough out or come by boat!

2. Cumberland Bay

Cumberland Bay is the piece of heaven that awaits discovery on St. Vincent.

Encircled by lush hills and stately palm trees, this beach embodies the essence of an untouched jewel of the Caribbean.

The Wallilabou River flows gently into the sea, there are occasional local fishermen pulling in their fresh catch, and people sipping on a few drinks at one of the quaint taverns.

A few additional locations, such as Mojito's Restaurant & Bar, are excellent places to stop and have a drink while taking in the views and beach.

Cumberland Bay has convenient access to parking. This beach is without a doubt among the greatest in St. Vincent, so there's no excuse not to visit it.

3. Brighton Salt Pond And Beach

Brighton Beach, widely regarded as one of St. Vincent's top beaches, is a vibrant location that has been rising up the ranks as a favorite among residents and tourists.

One of the first things you notice when you go onto the beach is the assortment of cheerfully painted benches and plaques with inspirational sayings affixed to the trees.

The double swing at Brighton Beach in St. Vincent is another noteworthy feature! It's undoubtedly one of the most Instagrammable locations on the island, painted in the colors of the St. Vincent and the Grenadines flag.

While Brighton Salt Pond and Beach offers calm enough water for swimming and paddling, it's also an excellent place to surf in St. Vincent.

Overall, Brighton Beach perfectly embodies St. Vincent's spirit of vibrancy, friendliness, and tiny surprises that turn a day at the beach into an unforgettable experience.

4. Mount Wynne Beach
Mount Wynne Beach, surrounded by the island's oldest coconut plantation, provides stunning views in addition to a glimpse of the past.

This untamed black sand beach, about 11 miles from Kingstown, offers excellent snorkeling, particularly in the vicinity of the cliffs to the right of the coast.

The beachfront area provides an enticing arrangement for a leisurely day after soaking up the waves. Three open pavilions with benches make this the ideal location for a picnic!

Don't go too soon, however, since Mt Wynne Beach is among the greatest spots in St. Vincent to see the sunset!

5. Richmond Beach

Richmond Beach has an unparalleled feeling of seclusion since it is the most northward beach accessible before reaching the La Soufrière volcanic region. Go to the road's end and park under the trees to enjoy the whole experience.

The beach itself has black, volcanic sand, and the lush green background and driftwood pieces highlight its rough character. The waves may be strong, therefore swimming is not advised here, but judging by the pictures, this beach in St. Vincent should definitely be on your list of places to visit!

Richmond Beach and the well-known Dark View Falls are conveniently close by, making this a fantastic itinerary for a day trip in St. Vincent.

6. Wallilabou Bay

Wallilabou Bay is one of the numerous beaches that St. Vincent has to offer, and it stands out from the others due to its unique appeal. It was near the gorgeous Wallilabou Bay where sequences from the Pirates of the Caribbean movie were shot. The movie set and props are still on the beach, despite the effects of time!

In addition to its association with the movie, Wallilabou Bay is a top beach in St. Vincent due to its calm and picturesque surroundings. Wallilabou is a well-liked anchorage in St. Vincent, where the brilliant, dark blue seas blend seamlessly with the black sandy coastline. It's possible to see a boat or two moored in the harbor.

7. Barrouallie Beach
Barrouallie Beach exudes subtlety without sacrificing warmth.

The settlement of Barrouallie, which was once a whaling town, is now its center. Local islanders are often seen cooking by the bonfire or "liming," as the Caribbean phrase for lounging, on the sandy beach. We suggest striking up a conversation and learning about the people' lives. The people of Vincentia are kind and want you to appreciate their island's beauty.

Additionally, even for a little period of time, participating in this genuine experience will leave you with priceless memories of your vacation to St. Vincent.

8. Young Island Beach

Young Island is officially a distinct island, but given its stunning beauty and close proximity to St. Vincent's south coast, it has to be on any list of the island's top beaches. Young Island is located about 180 meters south of St. Vincent.

With its immaculate white sand beach, the opulent and private Young Island Resort is located on the 13-acre island. Even though the island is mostly private for resort visitors, outsiders are welcome to explore, utilize the beach, and dine at the resort's restaurant and bar!

Go to the dock at Mangoz Restaurant and Bar to take one of the many water taxis that will transport you across Young Island to get to it from the mainland.

Young Island Resort offers complimentary 24-hour access to their own water ferry for guests staying at the resort!

9. Rawacou Recreational Park and Argyle Beach

Rawacou Recreational Park has two beaches, divided by a rocky headland and a breakwater that provides a safe swimming area!

By offering a place for leisure and enjoyment, this enjoyment Park opens to the public, demonstrating St. Vincent's dedication to protecting and promoting the area's natural beauty. Tall coconut trees along the beach contribute to the tropical atmosphere, and a man-made natural pool makes it possible to take a warm plunge. Aside from this, the Atlantic Coast's roaring waves make it the worst beach in St. Vincent for swimming.

It's the perfect location for a BBQ or an evening drink since there are many covered places, gazebos, fire pits, seats, and expansive spaces to explore. Rawacou is a must-visit beach in St. Vincent since there's always something to do there, whether you're exploring the coastline or just strolling about.

10. Indian Bay Beach

With its smooth white sand, Indian Bay Beach, which is in St. Vincent's southwest corner, is a noticeable location. This beach has a brighter shoreline than many of the volcanic black sand beaches on the island.

Indian Bay is one of the nicest beaches in St. Vincent close to the cruise port, drawing visitors seeking white sand and crystal-clear seas because of its handy location next to multiple hotels and popularity.

The view to the south, which includes Young Island and Bequia, is lovely while you unwind on the beach.

After your time at the beach, there are many eateries in the area where you can get something to eat!

11. Chateaubelair Beach

Located on the Leeward coast, Chateaubelair is a fishing community that provides visitors with a lively local experience and an opportunity to see island life in action.

The colorful fishing boats tied along the sand and the kids playing nearby show that residents use the beach more often than visitors do.

Make sure to include Chateaubelair in your list of beaches in St. Vincent. It honors the customs and sense of camaraderie of the island.

12. Coconut Grove Beach Club

Let's take a closer look at our last beach choice, Coconut Grove Beach Club, the newest beachfront jewel in St. Vincent and the Grenadines, with its white sands and contemporary beach club vibe. This completes our tour of the beaches St. Vincent has to offer.

This charming beach club has plenty of Instagram-worthy moments, a contemporary outdoor restaurant, and gorgeous palm trees—especially on the iconic large yellow chair! It's a fantastic option for beaches in St. Vincent close to the cruise terminal since it's just 20 minutes from Kingstown.

The meal menu at the beach club is excellent and fairly priced, and the beverage selection is also superb.

The clubby mood (they often have live DJs spinning records) and imported white sand may take away from the authentically local experience, but overall, the beach is worth adding to your list of St. Vincent beaches on Vincent.

The beaches of St reflect the island's volcanic nature, its historical importance, and its inhabitants. These beaches in St. Vincent are located away from the commercialized tourist routes and provide unique, off-the-beaten-path experiences.

St. Vincent offers a tranquil and amazing beach experience, whether you're looking for the greatest beaches close to the cruise port or exploring its hidden treasures.

Snorkeling and Diving Spots

St. Vincent and the Grenadines is a group of beautiful Caribbean islands that provide snorkelers the opportunity to see some of the most abundant marine life.

Saint Vincent and the Grenadines is a beautiful island chain located in the southern part of the Lesser Antilles arc, surrounded by the brilliant blue seas of the Caribbean. This paradise, which is made up of the main island of Saint Vincent as well as many other islands and cays (the biggest of which are Bequia, Canouan, Mayreau, and Union Island), is a sanctuary for robust reefs and marine biodiversity and is thus brimming with great places for snorkeling. Known affectionately as the "Critter Capital of the Caribbean," St. Vincent and the Grenadines as a whole are home to some 65 square miles of coral reefs, teeming with 400 different kinds of reef fish among an abundance of underwater vegetation.

While snorkeling off the beach isn't especially well-known in this Caribbean archipelago, some of its most stunning locations are accessible by boat, and there are plenty of trips available for those who want to explore the submerged worlds of these islands. It goes without saying that boat cruises are essential to discover the SVG islands' spectacular barrier reefs, immaculate coastlines, and picture-perfect beaches.

Furthermore, this unappreciated treasure is the ultimate off-the-beaten-path getaway perfect for travelers seeking a crowd-free holiday in unspoiled beauty, since it is one of the Caribbean's less-traveled islands. It will be worthwhile to spend the time learning about the top snorkeling spots in St. Vincent and the Grenadines before that ideal vacation, after the toes are sandy, the hair is crispy and salty, the warm tropical wind is blowing, and the reefs are teeming before the eyes.

1. The Bay of Wallilabou

Wallilabou Bay has the distinction of being the top location for beach snorkeling on St. Vincent's main island. Fans of the Pirates of the Caribbean films may even recognize its bay, since many sequences were filmed here (even more incentive to cross this location off your bucket list). Thanks to the excellent snorkel sites right off the shore, even people who have never heard of Jack Sparrow, Captain Barbossa, or Davey Jones will have their curiosity fully piqued. From a variety of colorful corals, gorgonians, and sponges to firework-like displays of tropical fish below the water's surface, this sensational section of the island appeals to discerning nature lovers as well as filmmakers.

In addition, some swimmers to keep an eye out for include bluehead wrasse, damselfish, trumpetfish, moray eels, and blue tangs, which are often seen frolicking amongst the rocky seabeds and reefs. When you combine the wacky rock formations and sheer cliffs that provide an amazing background for snorkeling in the sea, Wallilabou Bay is nothing short of a dream come true.

2. The Mayreau

Mayreau island, which is part of the Tobago Cays Marine Park, is a haven for snorkelers and scuba divers. The fairytale underwater world here has several excellent dive and snorkel spots, but one of the most remarkable to call home is Mayreau Gardens, a kaleidoscope reef teeming with life. This amazing underwater ecosystem is home to a plethora of creatures that snorkelers and scuba divers would be thrilled to see in this region of the Caribbean. Rainbow-hued coral gardens, vividly colored sponges, clouds of tropical fish, marine snails, and sharks are just a few of the bigger boys.

If an underwater enthusiast wants to explore the parts of Mayreau Gardens that are not readily accessible by swimming, a boat excursion might be the best course of action. Fringing reefs can also be found close to the beaches on the northeastern coast of Mayreau Island. Furthermore, travelers to this part of St. Vincent and the Grenadines get the best of both worlds: Mayreau, home to some of the most breathtaking beaches and marine reefs in the Caribbean, is without a doubt the finest place to go snorkeling or scuba diving and spend a day at the beach. Some of the most stunning beaches provide vistas worthy of a computer screen saver, such Windward Bay, Saline Bay, and Salt Whistle Bay.

3. The Canouan

Canouan Island, which is in the southern Grenadines, stands out from the rest because it offers some of the greatest shore snorkeling the whole archipelago has to offer. The ocean conditions here are excellent for swimming and snorkeling, with calm, clear seas perfect for seeing all the bustling undersea life living inside. The area is home to a mile-long reef that protects the shore.

Numerous reef fish, unusual brain corals, and other fascinating animals to see and appreciate are among the many marine species that are abundant in this area. Furthermore, Canouan Island's appeal resides in its accessibility and ability to accommodate overnight stays for those who are unable to leave after being mesmerized by its majesty. If visitors so want, they may extend their stay and make a whole additional day of their holiday at one of the many resorts and lodging options on the island; if not, they can always take a boat ride for a day of exploring.

4. The Cays of Tobago

The Tobago Cays, which consist of five uninhabited islands (Baradal, Petit Rameau, Petit Bateau, Petit Tabac, and Jamesby) are exquisite and covered in a vast network of coral reefs. The waters here are completely protected since they are a part of the 1,400-acre Tobago Cays Marine Park, which offers some of the best snorkeling spots in the whole Caribbean. The 2.5-mile Horseshoe Reef, which encircles the little islands located here, is one of the greatest locations overall.

A snorkeling excursion to the Tobago Cays will be very rewarding, as the marine life there is nothing short of breathtaking. From beautiful corals and sea fans to turtles, eagle rays, nurse sharks, and an array of reef fish, there is plenty to see and appreciate. Though there are several day excursions, guided tours, and catamaran cruises that provide access from St. Vincent and its other little sister islands, such Bequia, Canouan, and Union, tourists should be aware that these cays are only accessible by water. Another practical way to get to the Tobago Cays is via water taxi, which departs from Union, Canouan, Mayreau.

5. Petit St. Vincent

Located close to Grenada's sister island, Carriacou, Petit St. Vincent is one of the southernmost islands in the Grenadines. The island is privately owned and runs as a resort. Its 115 acres of tranquil terrain provide one of the most opulent and exclusive tropical getaways in the Caribbean. Not only is the island a luxurious haven hidden away in complete seclusion, but it's also a well-known destination for scuba diving and snorkeling, with many amazing snorkeling spots just off the shore.

There is an abundance of diversity to see in the teeming seas of this little speck of the Grenadines, from immaculate corals to richnesses of tropical marine life, including sea turtles, eagle rays, and colorful fish. Surprisingly, the resort here grows elkhorn and staghorn corals in an artificial coral garden as part of its marine conservation efforts. The icing on the cake for this little slice of paradise is that Petit St. Vincent offers amazing water sports and in-water activities that range from heart-stopping to soothing, with guests able to enjoy paddle-boasting, kite surfing, kayaking, windsurfing, sailing, and, of course, scuba diving.

6. Island Palm

In addition to being a paradisiacal island, Palm Island is a stunning private island that is only accessible by visitors of the surrounding opulent villas and Palm Island Resort and Spa. This peaceful island has bright white sand beaches that are surrounded by clear, shallow waters that are ideal for beginning swimmers and snorkelers to discover their fins. Although Palm Island's ocean may be breathtaking, there aren't many corals or reef systems in it. Nevertheless, the abundance of vividly colored tropical fish and the calm, wave-free waters make up for the lack of reef, making it an ideal place for kayaking, paddleboarding, sailing, and other exciting water sports and wet activities.

7. Bequia

It seems that the biggest Grenadine Island will undoubtedly provide some of the most amazing snorkeling experiences in the Caribbean, but its claim to be the "largest" is a little misleading given its small area of just seven square miles.

Merely 10 miles away from St. Vincent, Bequia Island is easily accessible; that being said, despite its proximity to the main island in this region, it remains relatively unexplored and seldom visited. Selecting the top snorkeling places in Bequia is difficult since there are so many amazing seas to explore.

However, the location known as Devil's Table, where a shallow reef that is popular with snorkelers and scuba divers both serves as a productive breeding ground for an abundance of marine species, is continuously ranked highly among the most frequently visited hubs for marine adventurers.

Numerous little and large creatures, such as sea fans, spiny lobsters, octopuses, parrotfish, snappers, hawksbill sea turtles, eagle rays, and cute seahorses, have homes protected by this immaculate reef. The Lower Bay, located at the western end of the beach, is an excellent location for snorkelers as well. It is a relaxed sandy length that offers access to snorkeling straight from the shore. Industry Bay and Spring Bay are other deserving additions to the list of places to see if you're looking for additional locations for relaxing on the beach and snorkeling in calm waters.

8. The Petit Byahaut

Finally, but just as importantly, Petit Byahaut is located on the southwest coast of St. Vincent; it's really exceptional and deserving of much recognition. Situated near a paradisiacal lagoon that can only be accessed by boat, tourists may explore an underwater tunnel called the Bat tunnel (though Bruce Wayne is probably not inside, preferring to lounge in the sun on one of the moored luxury boats).

Not only are there expansive views and lovely above-water lagoon landscapes to discover and appreciate here, but there are also striking subaquatic natural formations that enhance the snorkeling experience. near Dinosaur Head - a gorgeous site near Byahaut Point - snorkelers may view the amazing 100-foot-plus tall underwater wall draped in colorful sponges, hard corals, and beach grass.

Sailing and Water Sports

Sailing and other water activities are abundant on the stunning Caribbean island of St. Vincent.

There are many well-liked activities you might participate in:

Boat tours and cruises: Sightseeing with Cass, Island Fever Tours SVG, and Barefoot Yacht Charters are just a few of the boat excursions and cruises that let you see the breathtaking coastline and neighboring islands. Additionally, you may take bar, club, and pub excursions like Lavaman or The Cariway to explore the local way of life and culture.

Scuba diving and snorkeling: St. Vincent is a fantastic location for scuba diving and snorkeling because of its rich marine life and coral reefs. With the help of qualified instructors and guides from Serenity Dive, Dive Antilles, or Dive St. Vincent, you may explore the underwater marvels.

Canoeing, kayaking, and paddle boarding: If you're looking for an exciting and energetic way to enjoy the water, give one of these sports a try. You have two options: either rent the gear or sign up for a guided excursion like Caribbee Watersports SVG or Siteseeing with Cass. At Petit St. Vincent, you may also attempt windsurfing or sailing aboard Hobie Cat, Sunfish, or Laser boats.

For those who like sailing and other water activities, St. Vincent is a haven since there are plenty of alternatives to fit every preference and ability level. You will find something to enjoy on this lovely island, whether you want to push yourself on a kayak, canoe, or paddle board, or just kick back on a boat tour or scuba dive or snorkel to learn about marine life. You may also enjoy the excitement of windsurfing or sailing in a Hobie Cat, Sunfish, or Laser boat, or join a bar, club, or pub tour to explore the local culture and nightlife. You will be astounded by the breathtaking landscape and the hospitable people of St. Vincent no matter what you decide.

CHAPTER 7. Cuisine and Dining

Local Culinary Delights

The island's rich cultural heritage and idyllic Caribbean location are captivatingly reflected in the culinary scene of St. Vincent and the Grenadines, which is a vibrant tapestry in itself. Here, food is more than just a means of subsistence; it's a commemoration of the past, a statement of community, and a harmonious blend of flavors that evoke the spirit of play and warmth in the sunshine.

At the heart of this culinary tapestry lies St. Vincent's dominant industry—agriculture. The abundance of crops that the island grows, such as arrowroot, coconuts, bananas, and various root vegetables like sweet potatoes and yams, allow it to flourish. A profusion of fruits, from the exotic appeal of wax apple and dragon fruit to the succulent sweetness of pineapple, are produced by the fertile soils. In addition to supporting the local economy, this agricultural abundance provides Vincentian households with a wide variety of nutritious and fresh ingredients.

The lush fields that adorn St. Vincent's landscapes tell the tale of a people whose livelihood is firmly anchored in land cultivation. These crops are important for more reasons than just food; they support Vincentian households and are ingrained in daily life and cultural customs. Its gastronomic legacy has endured over time, demonstrating the tenacity of a people rooted in their homeland and all that it has to offer.

The island has a small but significant fishing industry in addition to agriculture. Seafood could easily become a popular export, but for now, local households are the main priority. Every day, the catch is delivered to kitchens all over the island, adding the bounty of the Caribbean Sea to the culinary tapestry. This regional method of fishing guarantees the freshness of the catch while also encouraging sustainability and a sense of community.

That means that when you taste the cuisine of St. Vincent and the Grenadines, you're immersed in a story that has been passed down through the ages. It's a tale of agricultural abundance, of fishermen casting their nets in turquoise waters, and of a community that cherishes the essence of their culinary heritage. Each meal becomes a chapter in this tale, a harmonic combination of sunlight, joy, and an abundance of tastes that characterize the essence of this Caribbean paradise.

1. Breadfruit

Roasted breadfruit and fried jackfish is the national meal of St Vincent and the Grenadines, and no journey to this tropical island paradise would be complete without eating it at least once.

Though it comes from the same tree as jackfruit and mulberry, breadfruit has a taste similar to potatoes and is not found in Britain. In addition to being mashed with jackfish, it may also be mashed with coconut and banana leaves or garlic and oil.

With over 25 distinct varieties of breadfruit found around St Vincent and the Grenadines, you'll be spoiled for choice whether you're at a hotel, local restaurant, or traditional café.

Where to taste breadfruit in St Vincent & The Grenadines

At St Vincent's Breadfruit Festival, which takes place every weekend throughout August in commemoration of this much-revered local fruit. Events are free in an attempt to encourage tourists to consume the local products.

2. Madongo dumplings

Made from local arrowroot coupled with nutmeg and coconut, madongo dumplings are a specialty that you'll only find in St Vincent and the Grenadines.

This is primarily because arrowroot isn't cultivated anywhere else, with St Vincent one of the few areas that cultivates the flour for commerce.

Arrowroot is naturally gluten-free, so anyone with food allergies in your party shouldn't suffer.

Where to try madongo dumplings in St Vincent & The Grenadines

Madongo dumplings are very much an example of home-style Caribbean cuisine, rather than a delicacy that you'll find on restaurant or hotel menus throughout the island. You will enjoy a true, genuine flavor of St. Vincent and the Grenadines if you choose to sample them.

The greatest places to get these delicious dumplings are family-run restaurants or street food stands, or if you're fortunate enough, a native may ask you to dinner! It would be hard to top the real flavor of Vincentian home food that you will experience.

3. Beer from Hairoun

The Hairoun Brewery is located northeast of Kingstown and has been producing its name-brand beer since the middle of the 1980s. Hairoun Beer, sometimes referred to as the St. Vincent Brewery, is now well-known across the islands, so chances are good that you'll see it behind most bars and on most menus when you visit.

In terms of flavor, anticipate a light, pale gold beer with little head, and be prepared for your nose to be filled with citrus aromas. We believe this beer is ideal for the Sunshine Island.

And what does "Hairoun" mean in other languages? "Land of the Blessed," naturally.

Where in St. Vincent and the Grenadines can I sample Hairoun Beer?

Almost in every restaurant or pub on the island. As the sun sets, enjoy a leisurely evening with other visitors, sipping locally brewed beer and basking in the warmth of Vincentian hospitality.

You may also go to the brewery directly. It is located northwest of Kingstown. To find out whether there are any upcoming special events, visit the website.

4. Rum

During your vacation in St. Vincent, you'll sip on the finest rum, which is a mainstay in the Caribbean.

Rum production has always been fueled by sugar plantations, and despite the current surge in popularity of cultivating bananas, the locals' passion for the island's favorite spirit remains strong.

Produced here, Sunset Rum is available in many kinds, including the well-known Sunset Very Strong Rum, Captain Bligh XO, and Sunset Rum Punch, which is well-liked by both islanders and tourists.

Where in St. Vincent and the Grenadines may I drink rum?

Where should I not go? Although rum may be found all across the island, for the best flavors, we suggest visiting a nearby distillery.

Try Georgetown's St Vincent Distillers Ltd., a Caribbean institution since the 1960s and the maker of the aforementioned Sunset Rum.

5. Buljol

A Caribbean favorite, buljol is a salad commonly prepared with shredded cod or saltfish, peppers, tomatoes, oil and onions. There are many variations of this classic cuisine, which is often eaten cold and for breakfast. The flavors and ingredients vary according to the neighboring location, such as Trinidad. However, we believe they're all just as tasty and appropriately packed with regional flavors. A wonderful meal to have for lunch outside under the bright Caribbean sun.

Where in St. Vincent and the Grenadines can I taste buljol?

Nestled in the quiet Kingstown Park in the capital, The Grenadine House has put its own unique spin on the traditional by serving buljol inside a half-breadfruit. book sure you book your reservation with plenty of time to spare since this area is a popular one.

6. Callaloo Soup

For those of you who are health-conscious, callaloo soup is a local favorite in St. Vincent and the Grenadines. There are a variety of options available, including variants with beef, soup, or crab meat, and they are served everywhere from weddings and parties to street food stands.

The primary component is a leafy vegetable from the area, the specifics of which will differ across recipes. The essential components are garlic, onion, pepper, potatoes, and coconut milk. Other potential ingredients include cassava and yams.

Where in St. Vincent and the Grenadines can I get callaloo soup?

The second-largest Grenadine, Bequia, is often included in lists of places to get the greatest callaloo soup. For a taste of true Vincentian cuisine, try The Fig Tree, Coco's Place, or Green Boley Restaurant & Bar. In Port Elizabeth, there is a waterside location for Coco's Place and The Fig Tree.

7. Seafood

It seems obvious that the main dish of St. Vincent is seafood—these are islands, after all! A popular choice is red snapper, but you may also discover less common selections like mahi mahi, pilot whale, bonito, and kingfish, in addition to more well-known flavors like tuna, squid, octopus, and lobster. The cuisine is known for its fiery tastes, and you may often find dishes like spicy fish, fried and baked foods, and filling stews.

Where in St. Vincent and the Grenadines can I get seafood?

Of course, St. Vincent and the Grenadines is home to several restaurants with fantastic seafood; Basil's Bar and Restaurant in Kingstown is just one place to get top-notch fish.

Excellent red snapper may be found at 4 Shells Fish Joint in Calliaqua, a small, inconspicuous restaurant almost at the southernmost point of the island that is consistently rated as having some of the greatest seafood on the island.

Make sure to visit the town of Barrouallie on the west coast of St. Vincent on the first Friday of the month if you're nearby so you may enjoy the delicacies of its well-known fish festival. Sample some of the most well-known catches as well as some regional specialties. We doubt you will find another experience just like this one.

8. Fritters with Bananas

similar to your delicious breakfast?

You've arrived at the ideal location. Since bananas are a widely farmed crop in St. Vincent, it stands to reason that the island's cuisine features a lot of banana dishes. Because they're so simple to prepare with only flour, sugar, and oil, banana fritters are a favorite comfort food of Caribbean people everywhere.

Where in St. Vincent and the Grenadines can I get banana fritters?

On Union Island in the Grenadines, you may have mouthwatering banana fritters at the eateries near Chatham Bay (take the swift boat from St Vincent).

9. Roti: A flatbread stuffed with curries, potatoes, and meat, this dish is flavorful. The Indian immigrants who arrived in the Caribbean throughout the 1800s brought with them the meal known as roti. Around the island, roti is a common street dish that is sold at a lot of stands and stores.

10. Soursop Ice Cream: This is a frozen treat produced from the pulp of the soursop fruit, a tropical fruit that has a spiky green exterior and a white flesh. The fruit tastes tart and sweet with a faint citrus and pineapple flavor. A tasty dessert high in antioxidants and vitamin C is soursop ice cream.

11. Fried Plantains: Fried plantain slices are made by frying ripe bananas, or plantains, in oil until they get golden and crispy. A popular side dish that goes well with any dinner or may be eaten as a snack is fried plantains. Sweet and starchy, fried plantains may be dusted with cinnamon, sugar, or salt.

Popular Restaurants and Eateries

Food enthusiasts can find plenty to enjoy in St. Vincent and the Grenadines Islands, a nation with a rich and varied culinary heritage that reflects its natural resources, history, and culture. The nation consists of the main island of St. Vincent and a number of other islands together referred to as the Grenadines, each having unique charms and attractions. This nation has a vast variety of restaurants and cafes to suit a broad range of tastes and budgets, so you may find any type of eating experience you're searching for. A laid-back beach bar with a breathtaking view, a formal dining experience in an opulent resort, or a neighborhood street food stand with real tastes are all options.

Anchorage Yacht Club Dining Room and Bar

Boaters love the AYC Bar and Restaurant, which is open all day. Breakfast includes fresh-baked bread and pastries, followed by salads and sandwiches throughout the day, and an extensive menu with local seafood, freshly made pasta, and delicious burgers at night. Together with tropical drinks and a wide variety of rums, the cuisine features locally sourced dishes including lobster when available. Here, casual eating by the sea is the main attraction, and the bar is open until "the last man standing will not stand no more."

Mustique's Basil's Bar

Basil's Bar is a stargazer's dream come true on the ultra-exclusive island of Mustique, and not only at night. You never know who will be sitting at the next table since it's a celebrity favorite. The open-air terrace is covered with a series of roofs that protect customers from the heat and the odd rain as they savor freshly cooked lobster and tropical beverages. Attend the Wednesday dance party, Thursday happy hour, or Sunday evening jazz at 5:30 p.m. At the end of January, Basil's also holds the Mustique Blues Festival, which has live music every night for two weeks in a row.

Flow Kitchen and Wine Bar

You won't be let down if you visit Flow Wine Bar and Kitchen in downtown Kingstown for a drink, an appetizer, or a full dinner. The restaurant delivers a broad variety of small plates, entrees, flatbreads, sandwiches, and pastas, all of which are ideal for complementing with the large wine selection. The decor is pleasant, with flickering candlelight and soothing music. After you're done here, check out the sibling restaurants Bungalow on the Villa Beach boardwalk (for pizza) and Flowt Beach Bar at the Blue Lagoon Hotel & Marina (for drinks and grilled cuisine).

Happy Island

Happy Island is a little artificial island in Clifton Harbour that was constructed with abandoned conch shells. It's actually just a little bar where you can hang out for a little and enjoy some food, drink, and conversation with Janti Ramage, the happy creator, owner, and operator of the island. Ramage has varied hours, so be sure to call ahead.

Jack's Beach Bar

Jack's Beach Bar, located on Princess Margaret Beach right next to the shore, is the ideal place for a casual lunch outside or a happy hour on the terrace, or maybe both. It's a great option for supper as well, but getting there by landside is challenging since there are many steps and uneven, dark terrain. Anticipate regional ingredients served with a global flair each time you visit. Choose from the renowned fried chicken and the fish of the day paired with a tropical quinoa salad or a smokey barbecue sauce, blue cheese dip, or Mama's Hot Sauce. Jack's delivers up to two miles from the shore, so if you're having too much fun on the water, order anything from the delivery menu and have it delivered right to your boat.

Restaurant at Paradise Beach Hotel
Take in a picture-perfect view of Young Island and local delicacies including crab back, Creole chicken, grilled fish, and lobster fresh from the holding tank at the Paradise Beach Hotel Restaurant on Villa Beach, approximately 15 minutes south of Kingstown. There's live music and dancing many days a week, and the Friday night barbecue (dubbed "Grillin' with the Captain") is an island institution.

Café Sugar Reef
The Sugar Reef Café is a cool location next to the roaring sea, close to Bequia's extreme northeastern coast. For lunch and supper, patrons may savor nutritious, locally produced fare like fish roti paired with mango chutney

and papaya-black bean salsa, or blackened chicken and Callaloo lasagna topped with Caribbean spinach and rosemary. The fruit and honey are grown on Sugar Reef's estate; fresh food, meat, and fish are supplied by St. Vincent farmers and fishermen. The eatery even fries using coconut oil and substitutes coconut milk for dairy. It's more laid back during the day and more romantic at night.

The French Terrace Dining Room
Situated inside the Mariners Hotel with a view of Villa Beach, The French Verandah Restaurant delights patrons with mouthwatering French cuisine that is expertly cooked with a touch of Caribbean flare. Enjoy classic French delicacies like grilled beef tenderloin with Béarnaise, as well as inventive dishes like lobster crêpes and fish in green pepper sauce. During the day, views of Young

Island and boat traffic" provide a relaxed atmosphere for eating, while at night, candles and sparkling stars intensify the romanticism.

Restaurant at Young Island Resort

You can reach Young Island, the first of the Grenadines, from St. Vincent's Villa Beach with a two-minute boat journey. The Young Island Resort's seaside restaurant is open for informal breakfasts, lunches including a local curry buffet, prix-fixe dinners, and BBQ parties, catering to both guests and tourists. Enjoy the sea wind while dining on regional favorites like freshly caught fish and lobster while seated in an open-air hut surrounded by tropical flowers. Whatever you buy, be sure to combine it with the house specialty bread, which is cut tableside in front of you and comes in banana, coconut, cinnamon, white, wheat, and raisin types. Just be aware that, regardless of the time of day, reservations are necessary in order to dine here.

Bush Bar

Cozy and rustic, Bush Bar is a hidden treasure in the middle of the Vermont Valley, blending in well with the surrounding lush rainforest. Fresh and organic products from the nearby garden are used to make a range of beverages, snacks, and light meals that are served at the bar. You may take in the peace and beauty of the surrounding environment, unwind to soothing music, and converse with the kind staff and residents. The bar also provides guided excursions of the neighboring waterfalls and nature trails, where you may see the abundant wildlife and vegetation of St. Vincent. Bush Bar is the ideal location to take in the real Caribbean atmosphere, whether you're planning a family outing, a romantic retreat, or a single escape.

The Veejays

Veejays is a well-liked destination for both residents and tourists, offering traditional Caribbean cuisine that will entice your palate. The eatery is well-known for its reasonably priced, hearty servings, and delectable, fresh fish, chicken, roti, and bakes. In addition, you may indulge in a variety of beverages, such as unique cocktails and revitalizing juices, all while taking in the welcoming ambiance and vibrant service. Veejays is a cultural experience that highlights the finest of St. Vincent's food and hospitality rather than simply being a restaurant.

Dining Etiquette and Tips

St Vincent and the Grenadines is a Caribbean republic that consists of a large island, St Vincent, and a series of smaller islands, the Grenadines. The nation is noted for its natural beauty, rich culture, and unique cuisine. As long as you adhere to certain fundamental manners and guidelines, dining in St. Vincent and the Grenadines can be a delightful experience.

Respecting the regional traditions and customs is one of the most crucial parts of proper dining etiquette in St. Vincent and the Grenadines. For example, you should always greet your host and other visitors with a polite smile and a handshake, and use titles such as Mr, Mrs, or Miss when addressing them. Also, you have to dress correctly for the situation; particularly in formal situations, stay away from baggy or skimpy attire.

Being aware of table manners and etiquette is another crucial part of eating etiquette in St. Vincent and the Grenadines. For example, you should always wait to be invited to sit down and take cues from your host about when to begin and end your meal. Additionally, while preparing each dish, use the appropriate utensils and store them on the edge of your plate. Avoid reaching across the table, making loud sounds, and talking with your mouth full. Additionally, you should abstain from using your phone while at the table, smoking, and binge drinking alcohol.

One of the most fun features of eating in St Vincent and the Grenadines is to try the local cuisine and specialties. The cuisines of Africa,

Europe, India, and the Caribbean all have an effect on the diversity of meals that are served there. The most well-liked foods include pelau, a one-pot meal of rice, chicken, pigeon peas, and vegetables; roti, a flatbread filled with curried meat or vegetables; and callaloo soup, a thick vegetable soup cooked with coconut milk and okra. You may also sample some fresh tropical fruits like papaya, mango, or soursop, as well as seafood like conch, lobster, or flying fish. The regional beverages are also available for you to sample, including rum punch, a concoction of rum, lime juice, sugar, and spices, mauby, a bitter beverage made from tree bark, and sorrel, a spicy drink produced from hibiscus flowers.

One of the most essential recommendations for eating in St Vincent and the Grenadines is to be aware of the tipping and etiquette. Most restaurants and pubs automatically include a 10% service fee to your bill, but if you're happy with the service, you may additionally tip extra (10% to 15%). Nevertheless, you should always verify your statement before making a payment, as some places could not include the service charge or might impose additional costs for additional services or taxes. Additionally, be in mind that not all establishments take credit cards or foreign money, so be ready to pay with cash.

If you observe a few simple rules of manners and decorum, dining in St. Vincent and the Grenadines may be an unforgettable and delightful experience. You may maximize your dining experience in this beautiful Caribbean country by honoring the customs and traditions of the area, paying attention to table manners and etiquette, trying the regional food and specialties, and being conscious of tipping and etiquette.

CHAPTER 8. Cultural Experiences

Traditional Festivals and Events

To honor the island culture, a blend of contemporary celebrations and customary St. Vincent and the Grenadines festivals are observed. Every year during the Bequia Easter Regatta, the populace participates in a huge boat race to honor their island history. The yearly Vincy Mas Carnival is how the nation flaunts its ties to the Caribbean. The Nine Days Christmas festivities showcase traditional culture, while the Mustique Blues Festival effectively showcases current music.

The Mustique Blues Festival
London blues artist Dana Gillespie is the creator of this St Vincent event, which has been going since 1996. It takes place on the island of Mustique over two weeks in January and February, with a one-night trip to the island of Bequia in the midst of the celebration. It has been increasingly well-liked since its founding

and is a fantastic spot to listen to blues and roots music.

Bequia Easter Regatta

During Easter, a five-day boat race is held on the island of Bequia. Many worldwide professional and amateur sailors are drawn to it, and they compete on the Caribbean Sea that encircles the island. It is very amazing to see, and on the last day, there are massive festivities that go well into the night.

Vincy Mas

This is a classic Caribbean celebration with street festivities with dancing and music, pageants, and parades. It is the most popular event in St. Vincent and is held every year for two weeks between the end of June and the beginning of July.

National Dancing Festival

September is a busy month for showing off both traditional and non-traditional dance forms. Professional dance companies, community organizations, and schools all put on shows. Expect to witness inventive ballroom and folk dances as well as contemporary and traditional styles.

Independence Day

This annual celebration commemorating St. Vincent and the Grenadines' creation as an independent country in 1979 takes place on October 27. Because of their pride, a lot of individuals utilize the public holiday to celebrate in public at gatherings held in the community.

Nine Days Festival

This event, which takes place over nine mornings leading up to Christmas Day, is exactly what its name suggests. It is exclusive to St. Vincent and the Grenadines and represents a blend of Christian and indigenous cultures. When you awaken to the upbeat sounds of traditional steel pan music performed at pre-dawn street performances, you'll be reminded precisely where you are. Towns and villages all throughout the islands have fêtes and fairs later in the day.

Arts and Crafts

Visit the National Exhibition, the Christmas or Carnival Arts and Crafts fairs, and the unique events conducted at the Cruise Ship Berth to see the finest of Saint Vincent and the Grenadines' handicrafts. Discover an unusual assortment of beauty, utility, and whimsy, from oil paintings and conch shell galleons to egg shell mosaics and coconut helicopters, during presentations of the Island's Cottage Industries and Artists' Studios. You may also find books written by and about Vincentians, jewelry makers, carnival dolls, steel pans, goatskin drums, handcrafted clothes and shoes, and a range of wood carvings.

Many contemporary art pieces and traditional crafts are made from the fibers and flowers found in the island's grasslands and woods. See how hats, mats, slippers, toys, baskets, and images of island life are fashioned from bamboo, banana fiber, palm fronds, grass, and flower petals.

Other times, take quick strolls around Kingstown to see a sampling of the artwork, or visit the Craft Outlet in Frenchs or the new Kingstown Vegetable Market above.

Handcrafted apparel and shoes, produced from local fabrics and materials.

Goatskin drums and steel pans are two musical instruments used in calypso and soca music.

Books include history, poetry, and fiction written by and about Vincentians.

Jewelers, who produce magnificent jewelry from gold, silver, and gemstones.

Carnival dolls are bright, jovial creatures that embody the essence of a carnival.

<u>wood carvings, which may be little miniatures or gigantic sculptures and often include humans, animals, and birds</u>

<u>Fiber arts: hats, mats, slippers, toys, baskets, and paintings made from bamboo, banana fiber, palm fronds, grass, and flower petals.</u>

Interacting with Locals

Travelers seeking something more than sun and beach may find St. Vincent's Island appealing. Visitors may fully immerse themselves in a rich cultural experience that highlights the island's distinct traditions and history by engaging with the people. The inhabitants are renowned for their kind hospitality and amiable disposition, and they are always willing to share their histories, traditions, and food with inquisitive visitors. Engaging with the residents on St. Vincent's Island, whether it is via street festivals, learning a skill, or enjoying a home-cooked dinner, is a gratifying way to get a sense of the island's unique customs and community spirit. This Caribbean jewel

Show consideration for the customs and culture of the area. The rich and varied history of St. Vincent and the Grenadines is shaped by the impact of several ethnic groups and colonial past. By going to museums, cultural institutions, and art galleries, you may find out more about the traditions, festivals, and music of the area.

Act courteous and amiable. In general, the people are kind and welcoming, and they value tourists who express interest in and admiration for their nation. To break the ice and establish connection, a quick hello, a smile, or a complement may go a long way. Another option is to attempt learning a few fundamental terms and expressions in the regional dialect, which combines Creole and English.

Exhibit patience and flexibility. The laid-back and easygoing lifestyle of the islanders sometimes results in postponements, cancellations, or modifications to plans. You shouldn't count on everything to go as planned or on time. Rather, accept the island's tempo and savor the occasion. Along the road, you may come across a few unanticipated possibilities or surprises.

Be fearless and receptive. Travelers of various interests and inclinations may enjoy a wide range of experiences and activities in St. Vincent and the Grenadines. You may discover the islands' breathtaking natural features, which include immaculate beaches and verdant jungles. You may also sample some of the regional food, which combines Indian, European, and African flavors. Additionally, you may interact with the residents and other tourists by participating in some of the community activities, including the music festivals, the regatta, or the carnival.

Salutations and Amity:

People from St. Vincent are renowned for being kind and welcoming. Never be afraid to say "Good morning" or "Good afternoon" to those who live there. Grinning when you strike up a conversation goes a long way.

Local Stores and Markets:

Investigate the neighborhood markets, such as Kingstown Market, where you may converse with sellers of homemade items, fresh food, and spices. Start a discussion on the traditional recipes and ingredients found in the area.

Take Part in Festivals:
St. Vincent features exciting events throughout the year, such as Vincy Mas. Participate in the festivities, mingle with the people, and take in the dancing, music, and cultural shows.

Participate in Community Events:
Watch for neighborhood get-togethers, church services, or nearby athletic events. These provide fantastic chances to mingle with locals, discover community life, and experience the character of the island as a whole.

Check Out Local Businesses:
Explore local eateries, cafés, and pubs by venturing outside of popular tourist destinations. Engage in discussion with locals,

find out what their favorite foods are, and maybe have dinner or a drink together.

Go on a Guided Tour:
Choose to go on guided excursions with people who live and breathe the island. This generates chances for interpersonal encounters in addition to offering insightful information.

Discover Local Traditions:
Respecting regional traditions is crucial. Spend some time learning about etiquette, traditions, and social conventions. Being sensitive to cultural differences promotes good relationships.

Take Part in Workshops:
Seek for courses or seminars where you may learn traditional cuisine, dancing, or crafts. Engaging in this practical experience often

entails talking to people who are willing to impart their knowledge.

Opportunities for Volunteering:
Think about getting involved in volunteer or community projects in your area. This enables you to make significant relationships and significantly impact the community.

Guesthouse or Homestay:
Choose lodging options like homestays or guesthouses that provide a more personal touch. This offers a chance to interact with local hosts and learn about their everyday lives.

Recall to treat others with respect, candor, and sincere inquiry. Because St. Vincentians are renowned for their warmth, integrating into the local way of life is likely to create enduring relationships and a greater understanding of the island's culture.

CHAPTER 9. Practical Tips

Communication and Language

Ethnic dialects and a consistent official language coexist in Saint Vincent and the Grenadines. The major dialects of English, Vincentian Creole, French Patois, Portuguese, and Bhojpuri are among the many vernaculars available. As a consequence, the residents have access to a variety of cultural expressions thanks to these various communication channels. These are definitely consequences of the country's colonial past.

Aside from the fact that the original Carib inhabitants were of American descent, English has been widely used in the state because of its proximity to the Americas. 400,000 people speak it as their first language. From basic to higher education, it is the only kind of teaching that is incorporated into the educational system. It is also included in print, audio, and visual media under the national multimedia program. In official contexts, it is also spoken in both public and private offices.

Throughout the nation, Vincentian Creole is spoken as the native language. It was created as a unique form of English that was tailored for widespread use in rural regions. With 138,000 local speakers, its popularity has steadily increased. Its written form employs the Saint Vincent Language Code in conjunction with the Latin alphabet. It has some similarities with languages from the East, the South, and the Atlantic.

There is also spoken French Patois, which dates back to the French colonization era. Its speaker groups are few yet influential, especially its European ancestors. The names of local sites like Mayreau, Petit Vincent, and Sans Souci are among its amazing legacies that have been ingrained in the Vincentian vernacular.

Electricity and Plug Types

The electrical system on the island is complicated and varied, using several voltages and frequencies along with various connectors and sockets. In this article, I'll go over the key components of St. Vincent's Island's electrical system, including its history, benefits, drawbacks, and consequences for visitors.

St. Vincent's Island uses electricity outlets and plugs of types A, B, and G. Two flat parallel pins are present on type A plugs, two flat parallel pins and a round grounding pin are present on type B plugs, and three rectangular pins arranged in a triangle are present on type G plugs. Standard voltage and frequency ranges are 110/230 V and 50/60 Hz, respectively. This indicates that although certain gadgets and appliances can operate on 110 V or 230 V, others can only use one of them. Certain appliances' performance, like that of motors and clocks, is also impacted by frequency.

The colonial past, geographic closeness to neighboring Caribbean islands, and economic prosperity of St. Vincent's Island all have an impact on the sorts of plugs and energy used there. At separate points in time, the British, French, and Portuguese occupied the island, bringing with them their respective electrical standards and tools. Along with having comparable historical and geographical origins, the island's neighboring islands, Barbados, Grenada, and Saint Lucia, also share certain electrical characteristics with it. The island's electrical infrastructure was impacted by its economic growth as well since it had to keep up with the rising demand for power from a variety of industries, including manufacturing, tourism, and agriculture.

Both residents and tourists to St. Vincent's Island have benefits and drawbacks when it comes to power and plug types. One benefit is that the island's social and economic activities are supported by a comparatively steady and consistent source of energy. An additional benefit is that the island's many plug types enable it to accommodate various appliances and gadgets from other nations. The island's high power costs are one drawback, which limits certain people's capacity to purchase and use it. The island's convoluted and perplexing electrical system, which necessitates converters and adapters for various appliances and gadgets, is another drawback.

It's crucial for visitors planning to St. Vincent's Island to be aware of the island's electrical outlets and plug kinds, as well as to pack accordingly and take safety measures. Before inserting their appliances and gadgets into the island's outlets, visitors should make sure they are aware of the voltage, frequency, and plug type of their equipment. Travelers need also pack adapters and converters that are compatible with the type A, B, and G plugs on the island. In addition, visitors must be mindful of the environmental and safety risks associated with using power on the island; they include the need to disconnect unused equipment, prevent overloading outlets, and save energy whenever feasible.

Sustainable Travel Practices

Travelers may reduce their negative influence on the ecology, culture, and economy of the locations they visit by adopting sustainable travel habits. Several instances of eco-friendly travel strategies for the island of St. Vincent include:

Select eco-friendly lodging alternatives that minimize trash, preserve water, and utilize renewable energy sources. For instance, you may stay at [Bequia Beach Hotel], which includes solar panels, rainwater collection, and composting facilities[1].

Purchasing local goods, using local guides, and taking part in community-based tourist programs are all ways to support small businesses and the local community. One option is to become a part of the [SVG Community Tourism Project], which helps the locals and provides genuine cultural experiences.

Respect the island's natural and cultural history by abiding by the laws and guidelines pertaining to protected areas, refraining from littering, and exercising caution in both your speech and conduct. For example, you may visit the UNESCO World Heritage Site [La Soufriere Volcano], but be careful to abide by the directives from the park rangers and the [National Parks Authority].

Utilize walking, bicycling, public transit, and, where feasible, hire an electric or hybrid vehicle to lessen your carbon impact. One way to go across the island is to take the [SVG Express], a bus service that links the major cities and tourist destinations.

Inform yourself and others on the social and environmental problems the island faces as well as the things you can do to assist. For instance, you might find out more about the [Sustainable Grenadines Project], a regional program that encourages preservation and environmentally friendly means of subsistence in the Grenadines islands.

CHAPTER 10.

Photography and Filming

Scenic Spots for Capturing Memories

A stunning country in the Caribbean, St. Vincent and the Grenadines has many picturesque locations for taking pictures. There are many locations to explore and take pictures, including white sand beaches, turquoise waterways, beautiful gardens, and old forts. The following are a few of St. Vincent and the Grenadines' most picturesque locations:

The five deserted islands that make up the Tobago Cays archipelago are home to some of the Caribbean's most beautiful coral reefs and marine life. Sail, dive, or snorkel around the cays to take in the sights of the verdant hills and the glistening clear ocean. Tobago Cays is the ideal location to capture the splendor of the Caribbean Sea and a haven for those who enjoy the outdoors.

Princess Margaret Beach: Named after the late British princess who visited the island in 1958, Princess Margaret Beach is located on Bequia Island. With its golden sand, placid ocean, and palm palms, it's one of the most well-liked and stunning beaches in the nation. The beach pubs and restaurants provide swimming, sunbathing, and relaxation options. Princess Margaret Beach is an excellent location to see the boats in the port as well as the sunset.

The oldest botanical gardens in the Western Hemisphere are the St. Vincent Botanical Gardens, which were founded in 1765. They have a range of tropical trees and plants, including mahogany, hibiscus, cinnamon, nutmeg, and palms, spread over 20 acres. In a little aviary, you may also see the national bird, the rare St. Vincent parrot. The gardens are a vibrant, tranquil haven in the middle of Kingstown.

The British erected Fort Charlotte in 1806 to stave off French raids on Kingstown's port. Perched on a hill, it provides sweeping views of the surroundings and overlooks both the city and the sea. You may tour the museum, barracks, and cannons in the fort, which showcase the island's history. Enjoying the environment and learning about colonial history are two excellent reasons to visit Fort Charlotte.

The Atlantic and Caribbean seas are divided by Salt Whistle Bay, a narrow crescent of white sand on Mayreau Island. It is a quiet, isolated location that draws honeymooners, beachgoers, and boaters. The pristine ocean is perfect for swimming, snorkeling, kayaking, and relaxing on the beach while taking in the views of the neighboring islands. A charming and romantic location is Salt Whistle Bay.

Bequia: Among the most picturesque islands in the nation, it is the second biggest. It boasts a long history of boat construction and whaling, as well as a relaxed atmosphere and kind residents. Visit the Old Hegg Turtle Sanctuary, stroll around the vibrant town of Port Elizabeth, or unwind on one of the stunning beaches, such as Princess Margaret Beach or Lower Bay Beach.

Mustique: This is the most prestigious and affluent island in the nation, where royals and celebrities buy opulent houses and enjoy the seclusion and elegance. You may take a horseback riding excursion around the picturesque trails and beaches, eat at the classy Basil's Bar, or stay at the magnificent Cotton House hotel.

Palm Island is a private island resort that provides honeymooners and couples with a picture-perfect getaway. You may pamper yourself to spa services, take advantage of the all-inclusive facilities, or stay in one of the charming cottages. There are five gorgeous beaches on the island where you may sail, kayak, snorkel, or go swimming.

Respectful Photography Guidelines

A stunning country in the Caribbean, St. Vincent and the Grenadines has many picturesque locations for taking pictures. When shooting pictures, you should, as a guest, also be mindful of the local way of life, people, and surroundings. The following are some polite standards regarding taking pictures in St. Vincent and the Grenadines:

Prior to taking pictures of someone, get their consent. Some individuals may not want to be photographed, particularly if they are going about their regular lives, participating in religious rituals, or having private moments. Always get permission before snapping a picture of someone, and respect their desires if they say no. Additionally, you should refrain from snapping pictures of kids without their parents' consent.

Pay attention to your surroundings and don't trespass: Certain locations, such as private property, military zones, or holy sites, may not allow photography. Always heed the warnings and regulations, and refrain from going into or taking pictures of locations that are closed to the general public. Additionally, you must use caution so as not to harm or disrupt any part of the natural environment, including plants, animals, or coral reefs.

Never provide anything of value or cash in return for pictures: Giving someone presents or cash in exchange for taking their pictures might be seen as obnoxious, exploitative, or invasive. Additionally, it could foster expectations or dependencies that compromise the integrity and dignity of the local population. Instead, make an effort to get to know the individuals you want to take pictures of, establish a connection with them, and express your thanks for their help.

Do not use flash or artificial light while shooting wildlife: Flash or artificial light may injure or startle the wildlife, such as the turtles, birds, or fish. To photograph wildlife in its native environment, you should utilize quick shutter speeds and natural lighting. Additionally, you need to avoid approaching or feeding the animals and maintain a safe distance.

Tell the locals about your images and tales: Telling the locals about your images and stories is one of the finest ways to appreciate and value their culture. You may email them copies of your images or show them from your phone or camera. To understand more about their lives and viewpoints, you may also listen to their tales. This may lead to a fruitful and meaningful conversation that deepens your knowledge and broadens your perspective.

Respect the traditions and cultures of the people you are visiting: St. Vincent and the Grenadines is a lively, diversified nation with a rich past. It is important that you understand the local way of life and refrain from photographing anything that might be seen as insulting, offensive, or improper. For example, you should not photograph persons who are dressed in traditional or religious costume, or who are conducting rites or ceremonies, without their permission[1][2]. Additionally, you should refrain from snapping pictures of sensitive or divisive subjects, as well as military or political symbols.

Be imaginative and creative: St. Vincent and the Grenadines has a lot of beautiful places to shoot, but you should also strive to be imaginative and creative with your shots. You should avoid using cliched or stereotyped photographs, as well as copying or mimicking the work of other photographers. Additionally, you should refrain from utilizing altering software or filters that distort the authenticity or actuality of your images. You should make an effort to convey your personal vision and style while capturing the distinctive and authentic features of the nation.

Give generously and show support: St. Vincent and the Grenadines is a growing nation with a wealth of potential and problems. You should avoid shooting pictures of the locals that show them in a dehumanizing or unfavorable light and instead be kind and supportive of them and their communities. Additionally, you need to refrain from shooting pictures that advocate immoral or unsustainable behavior, or that exploit or commercialize the local populace or way of life. Instead, you need to shoot pictures that honor the nation's variety, beauty, and resiliency while also advancing its growth and emancipation.

CHAPTER 11. St. Vincent and the Grenadines in Every Season

Seasonal Highlights and Events

Seasonal highlights and events abound on St. Vincent's Island, adding to the island's lively atmosphere and diverse cultural offerings. These annual events, which range from customary festivities to distinctive festivals, provide guests the opportunity to fully engage with the community and make lifelong memories.

1. Carnival Season (January - February):
The beginning of the year symbolizes the exciting Carnival season in St. Vincent. Colorful parades, loud music, and extravagant costumes flood the streets during Vincy Mas, the island's major carnival event.

2. Bequia Easter Regatta (March - April):
An exciting Easter Regatta is held on the adjacent island of Bequia, attracting both sailors and spectators. The regatta offers exciting boat racing, beach party vibes, and live music.

3. Nine Mornings Festival (December):
In St. Vincent, the distinctive Nine Mornings Festival is a Christmas custom. Locals celebrate with street concerts, caroling, and the renowned 'Jouvert' morning celebrations for

nine mornings in a row leading up to Christmas.

4. Maroon Festival (May):

The Maroon Festival honors the Garifuna, the descendants of fugitive slaves, and celebrates the island's African ancestry. Traditional Garifuna music and dance, storytelling, and cultural acts are all included during the event.

5. Vincy Mas (June - July):

The highlight of St. Vincent's Carnival festivities is Vincy Mas. It features a series of activities such as calypso contests, beauty pageants, and the grand finale parade, making it a bright and lively cultural extravaganza.

6. Heritage Month (October):

Heritage Month in October honors the rich cultural legacy of St. Vincent. Events that showcase the island's culture, art, and traditions include performances, seminars, and exhibits.

7. Breadfruit Festival (August):

The Breadfruit Festival is a gastronomic event that highlights this Caribbean mainstay's diversity. Indulge in a variety of breadfruit-based delicacies, see culinary demos, and take in live cultural acts.

8. Independence Day Celebrations (October 27):

On October 27, 1979, St. Vincent became independent of British sovereignty. Across the island, Independence Day is celebrated with colorful parades, cultural exhibits, and patriotic festivities.

9. Christmas Festivities (December):

St. Vincent celebrates the holidays with a variety of festive activities, including light displays, Christmas concerts, and customary get-togethers. The island comes alive with the spirit of Christmas as residents deck their houses.

St. Vincent's seasonal highlights and activities guarantee a varied and engaging experience throughout the year, whether you're attracted to the throbbing energy of Carnival, the cultural depth of historical festivals, or the joyful ambiance of Christmas.

Conclusion

Discover the natural and cultural wonders of St. Vincent's Island, from towering peaks to small towns. Climb the crater of La Soufrière, an active volcano that dominates the island's landscape. Explore the green forests and gushing waterfalls, where you may encounter unusual flora and fauna. Dive into the crystal-clear blue oceans to see the colorful marine life and coral reefs. Relax on black-sand beaches and enjoy the sun and landscape. Visit Kingstown, the nation's old capital, and explore its cobblestone streets and colonial-style buildings. Take a trip through the West Indies' oldest botanical gardens, St. Vincent Botanical Gardens, to see the endangered St. Vincent parrot. Discover the island's history by visiting

Fort Charlotte, a stronghold built on a mountaintop with panoramic views of the sea and harbor. The lively market sells souvenirs and handicrafts manufactured locally. If you have more time, take a boat to the nearby Grenadine islands, which offer even more beautiful beaches and island experiences. St. Vincent's Island will captivate you with its beauty, distinctiveness, and charm.

Printed in Great Britain
by Amazon